The GLORY
of God
REVEALED

The GLORY
of God
REVEALED

The What, the Why and the How of the
Current Revival of Signs and Wonders

by

Andrea "Andy" McDougal

Original cover design by Sherie Campbell

Published by:

Andy's Books
18896 Greenwell Springs Road
Greenwell Springs, LA 70739

ISBN 979-8-9987460-0-0

Printed in the United States of America
For Worldwide Distribution

Dedication

To the Holy Spirit, the Giver of all revelation!

To my family. To my youngest daughter, Elizabeth, who paid a great price to see this book come to fruition! To my three older children, who also paid a price—Patrick, Kimberly and Kenny.

To our intercessors, who answered the call to prayer!

To the mighty host of the Lord's Body who have cried out for more of His presence, have sought His face and desired to see His glory revealed in the earth!

To the wonderful memory of Sister Ruth Ward Heflin, our mother in Zion and the one God used to release us into this revival of His glory!

Finally, to all of the Lord's great glory carriers, who have paid a price to see His glory released in the earth—no matter what the cost!

Acknowledgments

With fond appreciation and gratitude to the pastors, intercessors and friends who co-labored with us and welcomed God's glory into their churches, homes, meetings, conferences and retreats and prayerfully set an environment conducive to the moving of the Holy Spirit. To the precious saints who sat in our meetings week after week, wanting more and more of Him. It was through their hunger for Him that the Lord released revelation of His glory and confirmed His Word with signs following, by demonstrating His glory.

Contents

And Moses said, I beseech You, show me YOUR GLORY. Exodus 33:18

But [the time is coming when] the earth shall be filled with the knowledge of THE GLORY OF THE LORD as the waters cover the sea. Habakkuk 2:14

Even everyone who is called by My name, whom I have created for MY GLORY, whom I have formed, whom I have made. Isaiah 43:7

Behold, I am doing A NEW THING! Now it springs forth; do you not perceive and know it, and will you not give heed to it? I will even make a way in the wilderness and rivers in the desert. Isaiah 43:19

But to each one is given THE MANIFESTA- TION OF THE [HOLY] SPIRIT [the evidence, the spiritual illumination of the Spirit] for good and profit. 1 Corinthians 12:7

Arise [from the depression and prostration in which circumstances have kept you; rise to a new life]! Shine (be radiant with THE GLORY OF THE LORD), for your light has come, and THE GLORY OF THE LORD is risen upon you ... and HIS GLORY shall be seen on you! Isaiah 60:1-2

Thus you were DECKED WITH GOLD AND SIL-
VER, and your raiment was of fine linen and
silk and embroidered cloth; you ate fine flour
and honey and oil. And you were exceedingly
beautiful and you prospered into royal estate.
                                    Ezekiel 16:13

Give to the Lord THE GLORY due to His name;
worship the Lord in the beauty of holiness or in
holy array.   Psalm 29:2

Kings' daughters are among Your honorable
women; at Your right hand stands the queen IN
GOLD of Ophir.   Psalm 45:9

The King's daughter in the inner part [of the pal-
ace] is all glorious; her clothing is INWROUGHT
WITH GOLD.   Psalm 45:13

Let us rejoice and shout for joy [exulting and
triumphant]! Let us celebrate and ASCRIBE
TO HIM GLORY and honor, for the marriage of
the Lamb [at last] has come, and His bride has
prepared herself.   Revelation 19:7

The heavens were opened and I saw VISIONS
OF GOD.   Ezekiel 1:1

God ... came from Teman ... and the Holy One
from Mount Paran ... . Selah! HIS GLORY COV-

ERED THE HEAVENS and the earth was full of His praise. Habakkuk 3:3

Surely His salvation is near to those who reverently and worshipfully fear Him, [and is ready to be appropriated] that [THE MANIFEST PRESENCE OF GOD, HIS] GLORY may tabernacle and abide in our land.
Psalm 85:9

And all of us, as with unveiled face, [because we] continued to behold [in the Word of God] as in a mirror THE GLORY OF THE LORD, are constantly being transfigured into His very own image in ever increasing splendor and FROM ONE DEGREE OF GLORY TO ANOTHER; [for this comes] from the Lord [Who is] the Spirit.
2 Corinthians 3:18

Out of the midst of it THERE SEEMED TO GLOW AMBER METAL, out of the midst of the fire. Ezekiel 1:4

In appearance THEY GLEAMED LIKE CHRYSOLITE. Ezekiel 1:16

Then the cloud [the Shekinah, God's visible presence] covered the Tent of Meeting, and THE GLORY OF THE LORD filled the tabernacle! Exodus 40:34

Behold, THE GLORY OF THE LORD appeared in the cloud!   Exodus 16:10

For they shall be as the [precious] jewels of a crown, lifted high over and SHINING GLITTER-INGLY upon His land.   Zechariah 9:16

* Emphasis has been added in all cases.

Preface

What is the glory of God? His glory has always been with us. You can look at His creation and see His glory. The colors of fall dress the earth in His glory, and majestic snow-capped mountains display His glory. Look up at the heavens, and you'll see His glory. Every part of creation has a manifested presence of God upon it, and that means there's a glory about it. The glory is His presence.

When we go to a church service, we can sense a glory upon it. From the birth of the Church in the book of Acts until now, it has experienced varying realms of God's glory. There is, for instance, a glory that comes when the old hymns of the church are sung. It's not anything that we can see. And it may not be tangible, as we think of tangible, but it's there nevertheless. As we sing those hymns, God's very presence is somehow manifested in our midst.

Today, most of us sing newer, more contemporary, worship songs, and in them, too, we sense God's presence and His glory. Indeed, for most of us, these powerful worship songs seem to lift us into even higher realms of the glory.

When someone among us is healed or delivered, we sense God's presence, His glory. When His Word is preached, there is a glory upon it. The Holy Spirit is near, and we feel His presence.

These are all what we might call intangible manifestations of God's presence. They are not seen with our natural eyes or heard with our natural ears. But that doesn't make them any less real.

Today, however, something very different is happening that has caused some of us to re-examine our definition of the glory. It is not only the invisible or intangible presence of God; it is now often both visible and tangible. Therefore the Holy Spirit has led me to define the glory in this way: *It is the tangible and intangible, the visible and the invisible manifested presence of God.*

When something is tangible or visible, we can actually see it and hold in our hands. We can not only hold it; we can also smell it and experience it in other ways as well. In the past God's glory has usually been intangible and invisible. We knew that God was present, but we couldn't see any proof of it. Now, however, He is bringing us into a whole new realm of His glory by manifesting His presence to us in remarkable and unmistakable ways.

These days, it is not unusual for heavenly fragrances to drift our way, for gold dust to suddenly appear around us or for precious stones or angel feathers to manifest in our very hands. These are all visible and tangible proof of the very presence of God, and this is the glory of God that is being revealed to us today.

Introduction

Gold dust falling on us, then emerald dust, diamond, ruby and sapphire dust, multifaceted stones and pure topaz crystals appearing suddenly in our midst, the cloud of God's Shekinah presence with us, puddles of golden oil on our church pews and oil flowing from the hands of the people in our meetings, the sweet fragrance of the Lord becoming at times almost intoxicating, gold and platinum fillings of teeth and gold crowns ... these and many other unusual manifestations of the Lord's glory have been happening in our services in recent months. What does it all mean?

There can be no doubt that we are standing on the threshold of the greatest revival the world has ever experienced. As we stand in this hour with great anticipation, the Church, the Lord's Bride, the *"whosoever will,"* will soar on the wings of the Eagle from the edge on which we are now perched. We are about to take flight in the Spirit.

It is obvious to all who are observing current events in the Church that we are coming into a great outpouring of the Holy Spirit, a deluge of anointing that will now flood the earth with God's glory and with miraculous signs and wonders. This great outpouring of the Holy Spirit will bring us into another Pentecost and will give birth to a Church on fire. There has never been an hour like this one, and no generation has ever partaken of the things that are about to be loosed upon the earth.

As we move forward into this revival of God's glory that has begun to be released in the earth, we will experience even greater releases of His supernatural signs and wonders. New waves of anointing and of God's glory will now crash in upon God's people. We have only begun to experience the early stages of what the Lord wants to do. A tidal wave of revival is ready to crash upon the shores of this land, and indeed upon the entire world.

Days of signs and wonders, miracles, healings and supernatural workings of the divine nature of Christ are upon us. We have stepped into something that was destined from the foundations of the world. The Spirit of the Lord hovers over us, around us and in us, creating an atmosphere charged with the power of His eternal purposes. All we have to do now, it seems, is step into this realm of His glory that has been prepared for us. He will do the rest.

My own role in this outpouring began to become clear to me in April of 1999. I was preparing for a conference we were holding, when I noticed some unusual opposition in the spirit realm. I was suddenly encountering many adversaries and was finding myself pressed on all sides. At the same time, I could sense the Spirit of the Lord making Himself real to me as never before, as I sought His face in prayer. Then suddenly, His presence broke in upon me in a dimension I had never experienced before.

I had been saved and filled with the Holy Spirit for twenty-nine years, and soon after being baptized in the Holy Spirit, I had been thrust into the prophetic. I had known the voice of the Lord, His prompting and His leadings. I had even experienced angelic visitations. Still, I had never had the Lord break in upon my life as He did in that moment, and I suddenly found myself in a new dimension.

The Lord began to tell me that He was going to be doing some new things in our meetings. I sensed that this had nothing to do with me. All I could do was to step out of the way and give the Holy Spirit full rein. God was about to make Himself known to us in new ways. He was about to manifest His glory in our midst as we had never seen it before.

I wasn't sure what all this meant. I had experienced many supernatural things through the years—a cloud of God's presence in our meetings, supernatural oil appearing on my hands while I was praying for the sick, and even a heavenly mist that would occasionally fall in our meetings. These occurrences, however, had been few and far between.

About a year before this, the Holy Spirit had spoken to me and told me that He was going to dress the ministry, and some month's before that a prophetic word had been given in which the Lord said that He was re-dressing it. It had been dressed in grace, He said, but now it would be dressed "in grace and glory."

I would spend many moments wondering what this "glory" could be. How many of us, over the years, have asked God to show us His glory, not even having an idea of what we might see as a result? Just as Moses had asked God to show Him His glory, I began to ask God to show us His glory. We also wanted to see it and experience it. But what was it? As yet, God's "glory" was some intangible something of which we had no understanding.

When the day of the conference arrived, my prayer to the Lord was not only that He would show us His glory, but that He would also make us to know exactly what the glory was. I still did not know exactly what the Lord would do, but I was filled with anticipation. As we began the praise and worship service, it was clear that something was different. The Lord was beginning to make Himself known to us in heavenly dimensions. Whether we had stepped into the heavenly or Heaven had come down to us I was not sure. Whatever it was, the Lord's presence now filled the place where we were meeting.

A fine mist began to fall on us. It was so refreshing that there was no doubt that it was Heaven-sent. Then raindrops began to fall upon the peoples' clothing, their hands and their faces. Some of those who felt the rain hit them immediately fell to the floor in the Spirit. One lady said that the raindrops stained her clothes so she could never forget what the Lord had done for her in those meetings. The manifestations of God's glory were just that real.

Then the fragrance of the Lord began to permeate the air in a very powerful way. After that, fragrance after heavenly fragrance was released, as people were prayed for. Oil and water appeared on the hands of some. An infant had oil and water on his body. As quickly as his mother wiped it off, it appeared again. We were beginning to get a glimpse of the glory of which the Lord had spoken.

When Moses led the people of Israel through the wilderness, the glory was in the cloud which guided their way by day. It was in the fire that warmed and protected them by night. It was in the manna and quail that fed them. These were tangible, visible manifestations of God's presence with the ancient Israelites, and now there are tangible, visible manifestations of His presence with us too.

As weeks and months passed, at various times during our praise and worship or during our teaching of the Word of God, the Lord would again break in upon us and manifest His glory and His presence. He was taking us deeper, but still we sensed that this was only the beginning. There was much more to come. What a privilege! We were seeing *The Glory of God Revealed.*

Andy McDougal
Baton Rouge, Louisiana

Part I

What Is the Glory?

Chapter 1

The Glory

But [the time is coming when] the earth shall be filled with the knowledge of the glory of the Lord as the waters cover the sea. Habakkuk 2:14

As Habakkuk prophesied, he saw some future generation. He saw a people destined from the foundations of the world, a people who would receive a great revelation of the glory of God. That revelation could only come from being transported to the very realms of God's glory. Since this is happening today, I'm convinced that it was our generation which Habakkuk saw.

As he prophesied, Habakkuk could see that the knowledge of God's glory would be so vast that the earth would be filled with it *"as the waters cover the sea."* We have stepped into the beginnings of that revival of glory. The fullness of it has yet to be seen, for its breadth and depth are too great for our comprehension. We cannot yet fathom all of it. But as we move ahead, one step at a time, we are getting glimpses of this glory. This is a great privilege, for few have been blessed to know these revelations through the ages.

Habakkuk saw an hour coming in which a certain people would experience the glory of God. They would have revelation knowledge of the glory because they had been in the glory. And, beloved, we are the generation of which Habakkuk spoke.

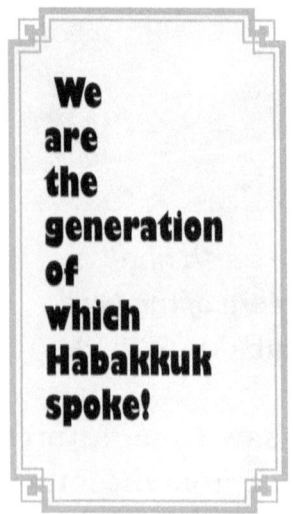

We are the generation of which Habakkuk spoke!

Suddenly, somewhat like thin onion skins being pulled back, layer after layer of revelation stored up for this generation and for this hour is being made known. And this is only the beginning. As we continue to stand in the glory of God's presence, we will not only see new signs and wonders, but we will also receive divine revelation of truths hidden until this hour. Now is the time, and they will be released.

The knowledge of the glory of the Lord will now flood the earth *"as the waters cover the sea."* It is not just the glory that will be seen covering the earth; it is also the knowledge of that glory, the revelation of the glory, that will come and flood the whole earth. What we are seeing is the beginning of it.

As I walked through a local shopping mall one day not long ago with my daughter, Elizabeth, I had to rub my eyes to make sure that I was seeing clearly. The Shekinah, the cloud of God's presence, was resting in several different areas of the mall over the people who were there doing their shopping. I asked Elizabeth if she could see what I was seeing, and she said she could. At one point I could not see it for a few minutes, but then I saw it again. This time it was resting over other groups of people.

This experience confirmed my belief that God's glory will not just be seen in our churches in the days ahead. It will soon be seen in our shopping centers, malls, airports, schools—anywhere and everywhere God chooses to manifest His presence. It will cover the earth. It is this visible glory of God that will move the hearts of sinners in the days ahead, and this revealing is what will result in the great end-time harvest for the Kingdom of God.

What we are now seeing is wonderful, but we are only in the very beginning stages of what the Lord will do. If He brought us into the fullness of it all at once, our minds and physical bodies could not receive or comprehend it all. The glory is being revealed step-by-step.

The Weight of God's Glory

This glory is multifaceted, and it encompasses more than we can presently comprehend. Our revelation of it is still limited. We have cried out to the Lord to show us His glory, and in answering our pleas for more of Him, He has released portions of His glory upon us in varying degrees. This has given us an excitement and an anticipation for God's tomorrows.

This word *glory,* according to *Strong's* (#3519), means "weight; but only figuratively in a good sense, splendor or copiousness." It is translated variously as *glorious, gloriously, glory, honor* or *honorable.* God's glory is weighty, full of splendor and copious. It is glorious and honorable.

According to *Strong's* (#4948), *weight* means "numerically estimated, the act of weighing ... full weight." One dictionary definition is "to increase in heaviness by adding another ingredient." In the glory, there comes a weightiness which many have experienced when God's presence comes into a meeting or church service.

I understand this definition, "weighing (the act) ... full weight," as meaning that as we are giving unto the Lord, through our praise, adoration and worship, as we stand in His presence under His anointing, He returns back to us a "full weight" of His glory and presence. We give unto Him, and He measures a return of full weight back to us.

I think of it in terms of a balancing scale. One side of the scale is full of our praise, adoration and worship for the Lord. This includes the singing of the "new song" of which the Bible speaks. To balance the scales, He measures back upon us with His glory the full measure of our worship and adoration.

I am not speaking here of God's grace, His unmerited favor, whereby He pours out upon our lives all of the wonderful things we don't deserve. I'm speaking of the realms of His glory. This is what we experience when our praise and worship ascends to God's throne room, and He releases upon us the spiritual rain of Heaven.

As noted, *weight* also means "to increase in heaviness by adding another ingredient." When God's glory comes into our meetings, or it comes upon us, or He takes us into His dwelling places where His glory is, more of Him is poured into us. There is a weightiness placed into our lives because He has added the necessary ingredients that keep us anchored, solid and secure, so that we are not tossed about with every wind of doctrine, not blown around by every storm that comes our way.

The Splendor of God's Glory

Splendor means "a great brightness of luster, a display of wealth or magnificence." The word *luster* means "the appearance of the surface of a metal as light reflects on it." When the glory comes, there is a splendor, a great brightness of luster, the appearance of the surface of metal as light reflects on it, a brilliant display of His wealth and magnificence:

But to each one is given the manifestation of the [Holy] Spirit [the evidence, the spiritual illumination of the Spirit] for good and profit.

1 Corinthians 12:7

One day I was ministering on this scripture in a meeting where the glory was manifesting on the people in the form of gold and oil. The word *manifestation* means "to appear, to show self, to render apparent." I was teaching that it is available to every believer. When the Holy Spirit manifests, or shows Himself, He makes Himself known; He is made apparent before us. And, when He makes Himself known, we begin to have an encounter with Him.

In that particular meeting there was a wonderful Catholic priest, and when I said that manifestation meant "to have an encounter with God," he jumped up out of his seat and with great excitement, said, "Can I tell you what else it means?" His obvious excitement produced an excitement in the rest of us, and we couldn't wait to hear what he was about to tell us. He said, "It means 'to have a brilliant display'!" He was right. When God's glory comes, He makes Himself known; He appears; He shows Himself. He is apparent and there is a brilliant display. All of this is for our spiritual profit.

The Fullness of God's Glory

Copious means "yielding abundance, plenty, rich, full of thought, information." This word comes from the word *copy,* representing the ability of great reproduction. In the glory, there is a copiousness. When the glory is present, there is an abundance of everything we need. The anointing is present in abundance. The healing power of God comes in abundance. His power to do miracles comes in abundance. Blessings flow in abundance, and supernatural change comes in abundance. Salvation is experienced in abundance, and the Holy Spirit is poured out in abundance.

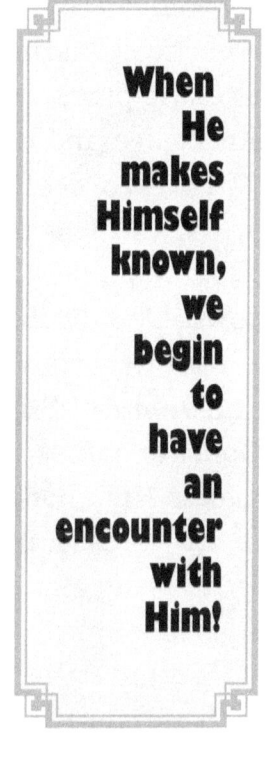

When He makes Himself known, we begin to have an encounter with Him!

In other words, there is more than enough of whatever we need in the glory. There is enough of what the Lord is doing to go around to everyone in any given meeting. No one need go away without having his or her needs met.

In the glory, there is richness to the Word, for revelation flows in abundance. When we are preaching in the glory, we have an abundance of God's thoughts, the information He wants to relay to His people. And when the glory is present, there is an ability to reproduce yourself in abundance in the lives of others and to bring about the reproduction of the Christ-like nature in those to whom you are ministering.

The Glory Comes as We Worship

This glory comes, or is manifested, under certain conditions. As we seek God's face, as we pray and as we praise and worship, it begins to happen. A heavenly dimension is released when we are in God's presence seeking Him. We are allowed to enter His dwelling place, as His Holy Spirit comes and inhabits our praise and our worship and our intercession.

The Word of God tells us that He inhabits the praises of His people (see Psalm 22:3). According to *Strong's* (#3427), this word *inhabit* means "to sit down," "to dwell, to remain," "to settle, to marry." It is variously translated as *make to keep house, return* and *remain*. Something happens when we praise God. He comes to where we are, and He dwells and makes His abode there. He actually comes and lives in our praises. In this way, He has given us the ability to bring His presence forth through the power of His Holy Spirit, as we seek His face.

We have the abiding presence of the Holy Spirit with us, as He lives inside of us and dwells in us. But when we gather together in faith to magnify His name, He comes to dwell with us in a very special way, to sit down with us, to remain with us, to settle with us, to marry us, to keep house with us and to bring us again, or return us to, the ability to encounter His presence. When this happens, the atmosphere is charged with His presence, His anointing, His glory.

The Glory Brings Provision

One of the first mentions of God's glory in the Bible is found in Exodus 16:7: *"And in the morning you shall see the glory of the Lord."* The Israelites had been murmuring and complaining because they thought the Lord had brought them out of Egypt only to let them starve to death in the wilderness. The Lord heard these murmurings, and yet He said that in the morning they would see His glory.

Sure enough, the glory of the Lord appeared to them the next day in a cloud (see verse 10), and out of that cloud God began to speak to Moses. He was instructed to tell the people that God was releasing their provision of bread and quail.

And there it was, just that easily, just that miraculously! As the glory of the Lord came in, that glory loosed the necessary provision for God's people. In the same way, we are now experiencing a supernatural loosing of provision for the people of God, and it is also coming in the glory. This supernatural provision will enable us in the days ahead to do all that the Lord has commissioned us to do.

Seeing God Face-to-Face

At one point, the Lord was very angry with Israel (see Exodus 33). In fact, He told Moses that He would no longer be leading the nation through the wilderness (see verse 34). Instead, He would send an angel before them. God was so angry with the rebellious people that He was ready to do them physical harm, but Moses reminded Him that He had promised to go before him:

And the Lord spoke to Moses face to face, as a man speaks to his friend. ... Moses said to the Lord, ...

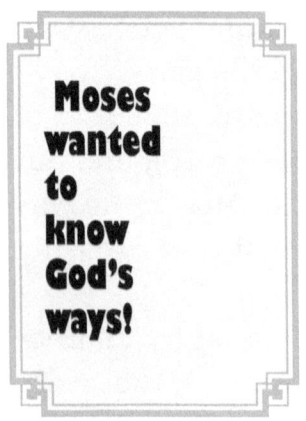

You said, I know you by name, and you have also found favor in My sight. Now therefore, I pray You, if I have found favor in Your sight, show me now Your way, that I may know You [progressively become more deeply and intimately acquainted with You, perceiving and recognizing and understanding more strongly and clearly] and that I may find favor in Your sight. And [Lord, do] consider that this nation is Your people. Exodus 33:11-13

Moses reminded the Lord of things that He had spoken to him previously, that He knew him by name and that he had found favor in His sight.

Finding Favor in God's Sight

If I have found favor in Your sight ...

Exodus 33:13

This word *"favor,"* according to *Strong's* (#2603), means to bend or stoop in kindness to an inferior." It is translated variously as *to show kindness, graciously entreat, show mercy on,* or *have pity on.* In other words, Moses was saying that if he had found favor and grace with God, he hoped that God would bend or stoop in kindness to him. He needed God's grace in that hour, for he was clearly inferior to God. If he was truly precious in God's sight, then he was asking God to move on his behalf.

"Show Me Your Way"

If I have found favor in Your sight, show me now Your way.   Exodus 33:13

Moses was not seeking God's acts, His miracles or His signs and wonders. In other words, he was not seeking God's hand. Rather, he wanted to know God's ways, His face.

This word *"way,"* according to *Strong's* (#1870), means "a road (as trodden); a course of life or mode of action." It is variously translated as *conversation, manner, highway,* and *pathway.* So it speaks of the road you walk upon, the course of your life, your mode of action, your conversation, your manner of doing things, your highway, or pathway. Moses wanted to walk the road the Lord walked on, to take His course in life. He wanted to know His mode of action, His conversation and manner of doing things.

He wanted to take His highway in life and walk His pathways.

"My Presence Shall Go with You"

And the Lord said, My Presence shall go with you, and I will give you rest.   Exodus 33:14

Because Moses wanted to know God's way of doing things and not just seek His acts, God blessed Moses and told him that he would indeed have what he had requested. In addition, God would also go with him and give him rest.

This word *"presence,"* according to *Strong's* (#6440 and #6437) means "the face," "the countenance," and is sometimes translated as *forefront* or *heaviness.* According to #3899, it also means "shewbread"—the bread of God's presence, the bread of His face, the bread of His life. Therefore, it is the turning of God's face toward you. When the Lord told Moses, *"My Presence shall go with you,"* He was saying, "I am turning My face toward you." I am sure the Lord was moving and revealing Himself in other places, but the minute Moses had a need, the Lord knew it and was there instantly. In that moment, the Lord, who had been focusing in another direction, turned His face toward Moses.

It is the same for you and me. As we seek God's face and not His hand, we experience the turning of His face toward us.

By seeking God's hand, we mean merely seeking His acts or His action. In this case, we may be seeking signs and wonders. God is calling us, instead, to seek His face. And as we do, He, in turn, is giving us signs and wonders.

Moses wanted to know God's ways, so he sought His face and His presence. He was not seeking the hand of God that would bring about signs and wonders. He was seeking the face and the presence of God. But, as a result of Moses wanting to know God's ways and wanting the presence of God, which is His face, God then showed Moses His glory, His manifested presence, through signs and wonders.

Many have accused those of us who are experiencing this current revival of God's glory in the earth of seeking nothing but signs and wonders. They are sure that all we want is gold dust. The truth is just the opposite. God's people have been seeking His face and seeking to know His ways, and because they have, the Lord is releasing His presence and His rest upon us. When Moses sought the right things, God blessed him with the turning of His face and with His rest.

"Show Me Your Glory"

And Moses said, I beseech You, show me Your glory.   Exodus 33:18

Moses only wanted more of God, not His acts, but His ways. He wanted to have God's presence in his

35

life. It is impossible to separate God knowing us by name, having His favor, asking to know His ways, having His presence and receiving His glory. These all go together. Knowing God's ways means having His presence in your life, and if you have His presence in your life, His glory will be there.

God's glory is a by-product of seeking His ways and His presence. Because Moses' motivation was right, he could ask the Lord for His glory.

"All My Goodness Shall Pass Before You"

And God said, I will make all My goodness pass before you, and I will proclaim My name, THE LORD, before you; for I will be gracious to whom I will be gracious, and will show mercy and loving-kindness on whom I will show mercy and loving-kindness.   Exodus 33:19

Not only would Moses know God's ways, have His presence and see His glory, but now God would allow Moses to have all of His goodness pass before him. God was not upset that Moses wanted to see His glory. In fact, there was a blessing in the fact that Moses wanted to see God's glory. All of God's goodness would now pass before him.

In this season of the glory of the Lord being revealed in the earth, we will now experience the presence of the Lord as never before. But we must always remember that it is impossible to separate

His presence from His glory. Because His glory is His presence, when Moses asked for the glory, he got the glory, and God's goodness came along with the package.

The glory is here, and the goodness of the Lord is now passing before us. The Lord wants to loose the good things of the Kingdom upon *your* life. He wants His goodness to pass before *you*, just as it did before Moses.

The word *goodness,* according to *Strong's* (#2898), means "the best, beauty, gladness, welfare" and is at times translated as *joy* or *go well with.* Jesus came to give us life and life more abundantly. He wants us to have the very best. He did not give us a heavy and failing spirit, but a sound mind and power. We were also meant to have joy, for it will be strength to us.

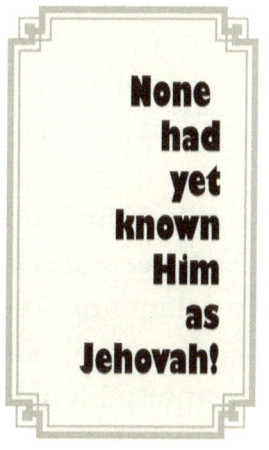

None had yet known Him as Jehovah!

God will always have our welfare in mind, and He desires that all things go well for us.

The Days of Awe and Wonder

It had always been foreordained that Moses would know God's glory and His presence. At the very beginning of his ministry, the Lord had displayed His awe, wonder and miracle-working power to Moses and through him as well. God's glory and His presence in visible manifested form were a constant in the lives of Moses and the Israelites whom he led out of bondage in Egypt.

God, in fact, revealed Himself to Moses, as He had to none other:

And God said to Moses, I am the Lord. I appeared to Abraham, to Isaac, and to Jacob as God Almighty [El-Shaddai], but by My name the Lord [Yahweh—the redemptive name of God] I did not make Myself known to them [in acts and great miracles].   Exodus 6:2-3

What the Lord was telling Moses was that He had never been known as *Jehovah* to anyone else before. To Adam and Eve, He had been *Elohim*, the Creator. To Abraham, Isaac and Jacob, He was *El-Shaddai*, the many-breasted One—the One who brought forth fruitfulness and abundance. He was to them the God of more than enough, and He blessed Abraham, Isaac and Jacob with abundance and fruitfulness. But none had yet known Him as *Jehovah*.

Now the Lord came to Moses as *Jehovah*, the self-revealing, miracle-working God, the God of awe and wonder. When He called Moses on the backside of the desert, He called him into what has come to be known as days of awe and wonder.

After Moses received from the Lord, God said to him:

Before all your people I will do marvels (wonders, miracles), such as have not been wrought or created in all the earth or in any nation; and all the people among whom you are shall see the work of the Lord; for it is a terrible thing [fearful and full of awe] that I will do with you.

Exodus 34:10

Where We Are Today

This is where we are today as well. The Lord now has a generation of people who are crying out to their God, Jehovah. They are seeking His ways. They are seeking His face and not His hand, and they want His presence in their lives. They have cried out to God to show them His glory, and He is responding— as never before.

We are learning God's ways, receiving the turning of His face toward us, having His presence and seeing His glory, and all of His goodness is passing before us. And just as He declared to Moses, He is ready to do marvels, wonders and miracles that have not yet been seen in all the earth. The peoples among whom we live in this generation will see the works of the Lord. These are the days of awe and wonder!

The Lord is clearly displaying His glory in the earth today. It is many-faceted, and it is being seen in differing degrees and through various manifestations. These are all signs of His presence being displayed in the earth. We are seeing *The Glory of God Revealed.*

Lord,

As we seek Your face and desire Your presence in our lives, come and show us Your glory!

Chapter 2

Created for the Glory

I will say to the north, Give up! and to the south, Keep not back. Bring My sons from afar and My daughters from the ends of the earth—even everyone who is called by My name, whom I have created for My glory, whom I have formed, whom I have made. Isaiah 43:6-7

These two verses of scripture portray a powerful move of God, a revival that has been ordained by the Lord Himself and proclaimed by His own voice. This move of God will release those who are the Lord's to come into their rightful positions for harvest.

The Lord speaks, He breathes, He whispers, and a revival comes into existence. All those who are called by His name and created for His glory are to come together into the fullness of His plan.

There are two colossal movements of the Spirit of God in the earth today, and they are colliding with each other. These are the former rain and the latter rain, and suddenly they are coming down together. There is another collision, a collision of believers— old and new. The newly saved are coming from the north, the south, the east and the west, and they are colliding with those of us who came to know the Lord in other times. Together we will form a people destined for God's glory.

There is no way that we can separate the coming harvest from the glory, and it is also not possible to have such a powerful display and release of glory and not have a great harvest. The two coincide with each other and are on a collision course.

The signs God is sending with this great revival are primarily for the sake of the unbelievers. We Christians don't need signs to believe in Jesus; we already believe. The current great demonstration of signs and wonders, the current demonstration of God's glory in the earth, is a demonstration of the power of God to the world. The greater signs and wonders and the greater glory that are on their way will be a powerful demonstration of the reality of the true and living God to a godless humanity.

The Former Rain

We have known the former glory. Each revival, each new moving of the Spirit, had a glory interwoven into it. The former rain represents all that the Spirit of God poured out in previous revivals. The former rain, the former glory, has come, but now we stand at the threshold of a greater glory, a latter glory, the latter rain.

In the natural, rain always comes to produce a harvest. In past revivals, a former glory rained down in various forms, and it produced a harvest of many souls. Now, a greater glory, a latter glory, is being released and is raining down upon us, and the release of this glory will produce an even greater harvest.

There is no way we can separate the coming harvest from the glory!

I am convinced that the gold dust and the other manifestations of the glory that we are currently experiencing are not the end result of the greater glory. These are just the beginning stages of a release of glory that will go far beyond anything we have yet experienced. This is only the tip of the iceberg.

Fashioned for the Glory

In the beginning God (prepared, formed, fashioned, and) created the heavens and the earth.

Genesis 1:1

According to the Amplified Bible's rendering of the word *created*, we discover that the meaning of this word is "prepared, formed and fashioned." So we can state that when God created the heavens and the earth, He prepared, formed and fashioned it into existence.

Bring My sons from afar and My daughters from the ends of the earth—even everyone who is called by My name, whom I have created for My glory, whom I have formed, whom I have made.
                                                    Isaiah 43:6-7

We see, in this particular passage of scripture that God created us for His glory! The word *created* in Genesis 1:1 has the same meaning as this word *created* in Isaiah 43:7. So we can see that when God created us for His glory, He prepared us, formed us and fashioned us for this express purpose—to experience His glory, to walk in His glory and to see His glory.

Yes, we have been created to give Him glory in all things. We have been created to glorify His name. But He has prepared us for His glory. He has formed us for His glory. And He has fashioned us for His glory.

This is a new revelation to many. When God created us for His glory, He wanted us to live in His glory, walk in His glory, experience His glory, carry His glory and display His glory.

What was long ago loosed in Heaven is now being loosed in earth. The things of Heaven are coming into the earth, and we are experiencing realms of God's heavenly glory. And all of this is because it is now time to show forth His glory to the whole world.

God is taking us into a new place, a place where the glory dwells. We know that one day we will walk on streets of gold, but right now, in this very moment, He is allowing us to walk into new realms of His glory, in the heavenlies. As we worship Him, we are walking into the dwelling places of glory, and His presence, His glory, is being manifested.

Framed for the Glory

By faith we understand that the worlds [during the successive ages] were framed (fashioned, put in order, and equipped for their intended purpose) by the word of God. Hebrews 11:3

All things have been established and put in order by God, the Creator. He has equipped us for our intended purposes. We have been created, fashioned, formed and framed for His use and created, fashioned, formed and framed for His glory.

This word *"frame," Strong's* (#3335 and #3336), means "to be squeezed into shape, molded into a form." As the potter determines the fashion, the form and the frame for his purpose, we have been created, fashioned, formed and framed, and there is a purpose to it all. We have been squeezed into shape or molded by the Master Potter's hands. The Potter has determined just how we should be fashioned, created, molded into form, squeezed into shape and framed for His use.

Webster's describes *frame* as "being fit for a specific use, to shape or form into a designed construction, for a purpose, for a particular usage." We were made by God and *for* God. We were created, fashioned, formed and framed for exactly what He wants to transpire in the earth. We are here by His design, and we are working for only one purpose—the ushering in of His Kingdom.

Just as the earth was framed for its intended purpose, God has also framed us for our intended purpose in this earth. Therefore we must make a conscious decision to step into the frame that God has designed for us.

> **We can choose to remain in the Outer Court, or we can press on into the Holy Place!**

We can choose to walk into those things that are of this earth and not of His Kingdom, and many people make that choice in life. They choose not to step into what the Lord has prepared them for from the foundations of the world. It is a choice. We can choose to remain in the Outer Court, or we can press on in to the Holy Place. When we decide to press in to the secret chambers of the Lord, it is because we have chosen the frame God has designed for us. When we choose to yield to His call upon our lives, we have chosen the frame He has created for our lives. When we choose to walk in the glory that He has created us for, we step into the frame of our divine destiny. When we choose the frames that God has prepared for us, our steps become easy.

There are many frames that you could choose to walk into in life, but believe me, they will not fit you as well as the frame that was created for you to walk into. Never forget that you were created, prepared, formed and fashioned for God's glory, for a specific use, a definite purpose. If you do not step into the frame you were created for, you will never fulfill your true destiny.

One of the benefits of the glory is that it comes to loose the destinies of those who are called by the Lord's name. Jesus said that His *"meat [was] to do the will of the [Father]"* (John 4:34). What this means is that the thing Jesus did best was to do what the Father had designed Him to do. The thing we will always do best is the perfect will of our heavenly Father. Nothing fits us quite so well.

There is a specific frame, a mold, that has been created for our lives, and we have been created to fit into that mold. No one else can fill your place. You are the only one who can fit into the frame God designed for you. Stepping into the frame you were created for, prepared for, fashioned for and formed for from the beginning of time will mean stepping into God's glory for your life, and that alone will bring you complete fulfillment.

It's Harvest Time

Isaiah prophesied that the Lord, when He came, would gather those who are His:

And it shall be in that day that the Root of Jesse shall stand as a signal for the peoples; of Him shall the nations inquire and seek knowledge, and His dwelling shall be glory [His rest glorious]!
And He will raise up a signal for the nations and will assemble the outcasts of Israel and will gather together the dispersed of Judah from the four corners of the earth.

Isaiah 11:10 and 12

This prophecy was literally fulfilled the day Israel became a nation. The Lord uttered these words, commanding the release of His children to come in, and when they did, Isaiah's prophetic utterance was fulfilled. The Lord, out of His own mouth, spoke to the four corners of the earth, to release His people and to gather His sons and daughters back to the land that He had promised them. And it happened.

The restoration of the nation of Israel is a symbol to us of the restoration to come in the Spirit. Just as Israel represents God's people in the natural, we represent His people in the Spirit. First comes the natural, and then the spiritual follows:

> *But it is not the spiritual life which came first, but the physical and then the spiritual.*
>
> 1 Corinthians 15:46

Paul was speaking in this passage of the first man, Adam, and of the second Adam, who was Christ:

> *Thus it is written, The first man Adam became a living being (an individual personality); the last Adam (Christ) became a life-giving Spirit [restoring the dead to life].*
> *The first man [was] from out of earth, made of dust (earthly-minded); the second Man [is] the Lord from out of heaven.*
>
> 1 Corinthians 15:45 and 47

Again, first came the natural and then the spiritual.

In his letter to the Romans, Paul wrote that he was not ashamed of the Gospel of Christ, for it was the power of God that brought forth salvation and deliverance from eternal death for all who believed—

to the Jew first and also to the Greek. First came the natural, and then the spiritual.

Before Isaac, the son of promise, was born, there was Ishmael. First came the natural, and then the spiritual.

The natural fulfillment of these promises has taken place already, but now the Lord, out of His own mouth, is commanding the four corners of the earth to release His spiritual sons and daughters. It is time for God's children to come in. He, the Captain of the hosts of Heaven, *Elohim*, the Creator of the universe, the Ancient of Days, the I Am, the God who was, the God who is and the God who is to come, the Alpha and the Omega, the First and the Last, is calling His sons and daughters to come into the Kingdom.

The earth must now obey, as its Creator speaks for His children to come to Him. It's harvest time, and the fields are surely white unto harvest. As we experience one of the greatest outpourings of the Holy Spirit the world has ever seen, we're coming off of the ash heap and beginning to dance like mothers rejoicing over newborn children.

Our spiritual children are coming in. The sons and daughters of Zion, those who from the foundations of the world were destined for salvation, are coming in. Mighty angels stand with sickles raised to harvest the grain from the whole earth. That grain may now be standing in the gross darkness of this world, but it is about to come out of the kingdom of darkness into the Kingdom of light, the Kingdom of God's dear Son.

If we could only feel the power of what is about to happen, we would all be much more excited about our tomorrows. Because we are on a collision course with God's glory and revival, great destinies will soon be released. Together, we are beginning to see *The Glory of God Revealed.*

Father,

You are speaking a revival into existence, and the sons and daughters of Zion are coming in. You have created us, prepared us, fashioned us, formed and framed us for Your glory! You have created us to walk in Your glory, see Your glory, experience Your glory and display Your glory. Help us to step into the fullness of what You have created us for and of all that You are doing in the earth.

Chapter 3

A "New Thing"

Behold, I am doing a new thing! Now it springs forth; do you not perceive and know it and will you not give heed to it? I will even make a way in the wilderness and rivers in the desert.

Isaiah 43:19

It would be very difficult for anyone to deny that we have stepped into a *"new thing."* It may not be a *"new thing"* to the Lord, but it certainly is new to us.

We had long known, or at the very least sensed, that the Lord was about to do something new in the earth. Over a period of nearly a dozen years, we had heard this truth prophesied, taught, read and declared. This had been even more true during the past year or two. In fact, it seemed that everything the Lord had me teaching was in preparation for this *"new thing."*

In one sense, God has always done new things. Pentecost was a *"new thing"* to those who experienced it. Being delivered from Egypt and having the waters of the Red Sea part was a *"new thing"* for the children of Israel. Later, entering the Promised Land and defeating the giants that lived there was a *"new thing"* for them. The Lord was forever bringing His people into some *"new thing."* Of course, none of it was new to our God, only to those who were experiencing it.

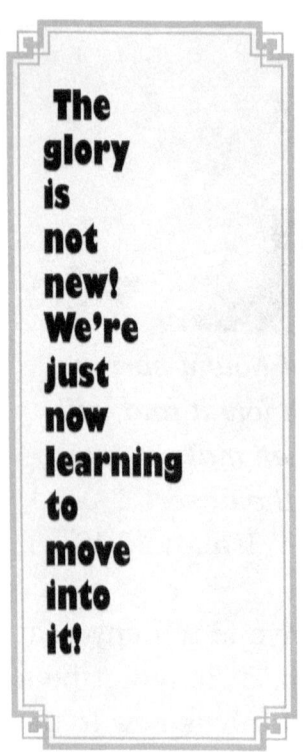

The glory is not new! We're just now learning to move into it!

In this sense, the glory is not a *"new thing."* We just have not had an understanding or a revelation of it until now. It has been available all along, but we are just now learning to move into it.

Not So New

The Word of God is full of revelation on the glory, and even of gold being manifested on God's people, so gold dust is also not a *"new thing."* Back during the Charismatic Renewal of the 1960s and 70s there were reports of gold dust manifestations and gold fillings. Experiencing the glory, for us, however, has been a *"new thing,"* especially with the gold dust. We had experienced the glory of God in measure, but encountering it in these levels has certainly been a *"new thing."*

When the prophet Isaiah spoke forth the words of Isaiah 43:19, Israel was just coming out of captivity in Babylon. He wanted to let his people know that God was going to do a *"new thing"* with them and for them. And it is the same today. The Church is coming out of captivity. Some would call it a "lull," a "lack of revival," a "wilderness experience," "the back side of the desert" or "a sleeping church." However you care to express it, we are now coming out, and our God is doing a *"new thing"* for us.

Stepping into the New

On Friday, December 3, 1999, we were in a meeting with our intercessors in Mandeville, Louisiana, when an amazing prophetic word came forth. We did not experience a bolt of lightning from Heaven, and the earth did not shake beneath us. This word from the Lord came forth with great ease and simplicity. He said to us:

Today is the day that you are stepping into the new thing. Today I am bringing you into the new thing that I am doing in the earth. Forget the former things. Forget the way things were. And forget your past failures. Today, I am bringing you into the new thing.

In submission to this word from the Lord, we joined hands and took a step, signifying that we were stepping into the *"new thing."* We believed that if we would do our part, the Lord would surely do what He had said.

As we took that step, we were not just stepping into a *"new thing"*; we were also stepping out of the old. We were choosing to leave behind all of our yesterdays, our past failures and our disappointments. Forgetting what was behind us, we were setting our faces toward what the Lord wanted to do in our lives in that new day.

That evening I had another meeting, this one in New Orleans. As we were worshiping in that meeting, a prophecy came forth. Neither the woman who gave the prophecy nor the others who were present had any idea of what had transpired in our earlier meeting that day. This is the prophetic word that came forth:

Behold, today you are stepping into the new thing that I am doing in the earth.

We decided to respond in the same way. We joined hands and took a step, signifying that we were prophetically stepping into the *"new thing"* the Lord had for us. There was no pretense of knowing exactly what the Lord was about to do, but everything was pointing toward something absolutely grand, and we were believing to be part of it.

About a month after that, I began reading Ruth Ward Heflin's book *Golden Glory* (McDougal Publishing, Hagerstown, MD: 2000), and I discovered that God had told her to do exactly the same thing and others had been led to do it too. How very exciting!

After we had chosen to step into the new things the Lord had for us, He began to catapult us into previously unknown realms of His glory. Revelation began to flow in our midst, but with it came the many manifestations of the glory: gold dust, emerald dust, diamond dust, ruby and sapphire dust, multifaceted stones and pure topaz crystals. Even the cloud of God's Shekinah presence was at times manifested in our midst. Puddles of golden oil appeared on church pews, and the sweet fragrance of the Lord became almost intoxicating at times.

Oil would flow from the hands of people in the meetings, and gold dust would appear on my face and clothes as I preached the Word. Gold and platinum fillings would appear in the teeth of those we ministered to. In some instances, the fillings were in the shape of a cross. One gold filling had a stone inside of it. And there were also gold crowns.

Perhaps as amazing as anything else, powerful impartation would come upon people's lives during the preaching of the Word of God.

A Time of Blessing

The day after we took a step of faith in the *"new thing,"* we held our regular weekly service in the Prairieville area, and we began to briefly share about this experience. One regular participant in that service could hardly contain herself. She reminded us of a message I had given on Yom Kippur (Monday, September 20, 1999), only four days from the Feast of Tabernacles. The message had been entitled "From the Ninth Month, the Twenty-fourth Day, I Will Bless You." I had declared that from the ninth month and the twenty-fourth day, the Lord would loose upon us blessings—anointing, the harvest, oil, wine and grain—everything that we had been longing for and eagerly anticipating.

I had said that everything was pointing to this reality, that we were stepping into "the third day" spoken of in the Scriptures and that this was to be a sacred year, the real Jubilee. If was, I had declared, the time the Lord had set aside to favor His people.

Because of how excited this woman had been concerning this message, she had gone home and done some research on the timing of the event in question. Much to her surprise (and ours as well), she had learned that according to the sacred Jewish calendar, the ninth month and the twenty-fourth day had been Friday, December 3, 1999, the same day the Lord had spoken to us declaring it to be the day of the release of the *"new thing"* upon us.

Not only was it the ninth month and the twenty-fourth day, according to the sacred Jewish calendar, but it was also the first day of Hanukkah, according to the regular Jewish calendar. Hanukkah is not only the Feast of Lights, but it is also the feast of new beginnings. The Lord was confirming His word to us by the mouth of two or three witnesses.

What Is the "New Thing"?

Is the *"new thing"* God spoke of only gold dust? No, of course not. The *"new thing"* is everything the Holy Spirit wants to do in our lives. Waves of glory, waves of anointing, walking in victory, fulfilling our destinies and whatever else the Lord has for us that we have not yet walked into ... this is our *"new thing."* There are dreams that the Holy Spirit has placed inside of us and promises that He has made to us that have yet to be fulfilled. The Lord wants to do all these things and more in our lives. He wants us to have the "new thing" more than we want to have it.

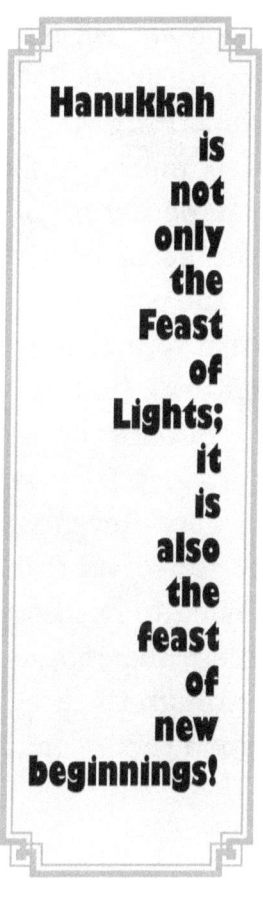

Hanukkah is not only the Feast of Lights; it is also the feast of new beginnings!

Part of the *"new thing"* God wants to do in each of our lives is revival, the bringing in of a great harvest, powerful anointings being released in the earth, signs and wonders and great manifestations of His glory—all for the sake of the harvest.

59

Coming Out of Captivity

Now it springs forth; do you not perceive it?

Isaiah 43:19

"Now"! As Isaiah prophesied these words, he was trying to let Israel know that this event was not something way off in the distance somewhere. This was important for their morale.

The nation of Israel was coming out of captivity, and Jerusalem, their beloved city, had been burned to the ground. There was nothing left for them to return to, nothing for them to look forward to—in the natural, that is.

Seventy years of captivity had brought the people very low. They were now lacking in power, vision and vitality. Seventy years is a long time, and the strain of those years had left them in hopelessness and despair. The Lord wanted to bring revival back into their hearts and into their spirits. He was, He said through the prophet, doing a *"new thing,"* and it was upon them *"now."*

Now Is the Time

The same is true for us today. The hour of our captivity, our wilderness experience, is coming to an end. The time is *"now." "Now it springs forth."* The Lord is delivering us out of our captivity, making a way for us in the wilderness and bringing streams of living water into the deserts of our lives. Now we are ready to enter our Promised Land.

God wants to pour out His Spirit upon all flesh. He wants to flood the earth with the manifestation of a realm of His glory that has never been seen before. We must be willing to step into all that He has for us.

Forgetting the Past

Just before this, Isaiah had said:

Do not [earnestly] remember the former things; neither consider the things of old.
Isaiah 43:18

God is definitely doing a "new thing," and we will have to step into it, not looking back or remembering the way He moved in the past. In other words, we can't box God in to doing it the way we have seen Him do things in the past.

I remembered something I had often heard Pastor Bill Buck say. Back in the early 1990s, I was serving as a missionary to Mexico and was on staff as Music Minister at the Church at El Paso, in El Paso, Texas, with pastors Bill and Elsie Buck. The Lord had used that couple to spark the Charismatic Movement throughout the entire Southwest region, from the southern tip of the Rocky Mountains to the northern tip.

Many times I heard Pastor Bill say that because he had been used in the Charismatic Renewal, he might be more prone to miss the next great move of God or to find it difficult to embrace. This was something that concerned him, because he did not want to miss what God was about to do, and for that reason, he kept himself open to what God was currently doing in the earth.

He pointed out that those who had been used in previous revivals were often the first to reject new things. Their stance would be, "God didn't move like this in the revival we experienced, so this certainly cannot be from Him." Many have missed new things that came along because of a similar attitude.

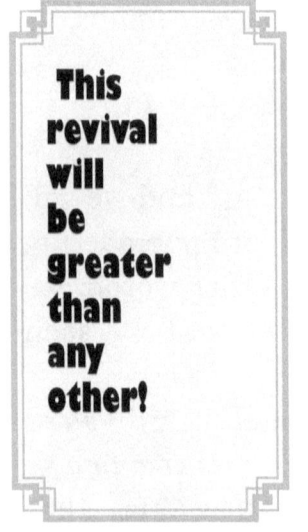

This revival will be greater than any other!

Don't Miss What God Has for You

This clearly presents a danger. So, if we have been used in previous revivals, let us not miss this new one that is coming. This will be the greatest revival yet. This will be the former rain and the latter rain together. It will be the culmination of all the revivals that have ever come upon the earth. How sad it would be to miss it because of preconceived ideas of how God can move! Let us embrace the "new thing" with open hearts and open minds, lest we miss our greatest and grandest hour.

A "New Thing"

The coming of the former rain and the latter rain together represents a scooping up of all of that took place in the revivals of the past and combining it with something totally new. It is like taking the third-hour anointing, the sixth-hour anointing and the ninth-hour anointing and adding to that mixture a last-hour anointing. This anointing cannot be left out of the mix, because this revival will be greater than any other.

"It's Not for Today"

In His time on earth, Jesus fulfilled each of the feasts except one—Tabernacles. Many have entered into Passover, passing over from a sin-filled life into salvation. When Pentecost (the baptism of the Holy Spirit) came to our day and time, many said (and still are saying) that it was not for today. People like that have missed Pentecost, missed the promise, the gift and the blessing of having the power of the Holy Spirit with the evidence of speaking in tongues. They have remained locked into Passover.

In the same way, many will also find themselves incapable of accepting this next move of God that is coming. Some of them will remain locked into Pentecost, insisting that Tabernacles is "not for today." As a result, they will miss the greatest outpouring of God's Spirit the world has ever seen. At any cost, we must embrace what the Lord is doing in the earth, for our day of visitation is upon us!

A Prayer for Revival

A prayer of Habakkuk the prophet, set to wild, enthusiastic, and triumphal music. O Lord, I have heard the report of You and was afraid. O Lord, revive Your work in the midst of the years, in the midst of the years make [Yourself] known! In wrath [earnestly] remember love, pity, and mercy.   Habakkuk 3:1-2

The Lord raised up a dreadful and terrible people to bring His disobedient sons into bondage because of their sin and rebellion. During their seventy years of captivity, there was no real move of God among them. Everyday life went on, and it was "business as usual." Then Habakkuk prayed this prophetic prayer, set to *"wild, enthusiastic, and triumphal music."* I can just see it now.

This reminds me of a young prophet I once met. He was also wild and enthusiastic as he sang, preached, prophesied, shouted and taught, and everything he did rhymed and was accompanied by wild and enthusiastic music. He was another Habakkuk, and we need some more of them today.

Nothing of interest had been taking place in Habakkuk's time. There was no revival, no glory, no signs and wonders, no great move of God. But as he prayed with prophetic unction, backed up by powerful music, something began to happen.

Habakkuk cried out, *"O Lord, I have heard the report of You and was afraid."* In other words, "I have heard how You moved in bygone days. I have heard how You parted the Red Sea and delivered Your people with Your mighty right arm out of Egypt. I heard how You gave Your people manna in the wilderness. I heard how You brought the days of awe and wonder with Moses and Joshua, and how Your people visibly saw Your glory. I heard how You raised up deliverers to set Your people free and bring revival to the land. O Lord, I have heard of all Your wondrous works!"

Lord, Come and Do It Again!

Then Habakkuk cried, *"O Lord, revive Your work in the midst of the years, in the midst of the years make Yourself known!"* He was saying, "Lord, will You do it again? Revive Your work! Lord, there are things that used to happen that are not happening anymore. There are things that have been bound up. Loose them, Lord! Right in the middle of these years, revive Your work: Raise up deliverers, bring revival, let us see Your glory, bring the days of awe and wonder again. Your people need a new Red Sea miracle. Your people want to cross the Jordan and enter their Promised Land. There are many things that have been held in reserve. O Lord, bring them out of storage, and make Yourself known in the earth as you did before."

And the Lord is doing just that today. He is reviving His work in the midst of the years. Right now, in our time, He is pulling out of storage, if you will, the days of awe and wonder—the miraculous. He is allowing us to see things we have never seen and to experience things we have never experienced.

The mighty works of our God are coming out of storage. They have been reserved for such a time as this. They have been preserved for a generation that, at a set time, God would favor. Why? Because He wants to fulfill His ultimate purpose and design in the earth. He is reviving His work in the midst of the years to fulfill His Word. And, in so doing, He is bringing the Church into her grandest hour. Thank God that we are now beginning to witness *The Glory of God Revealed.*

Lord,

We choose not to look at how You brought revival in the past or the way You moved in our lives in other times. Help us to embrace the moving of Your Spirit in this hour and to accept the "new thing" You are doing in the earth. And, Lord, reveal the things that have been in storage, things that have been held in reserve, waiting for this generation!

Chapter 4

Arise and Shine

Arise, shine; for thy light is come, and the glory of the LORD is risen upon thee.
Isaiah 60:1, KJV

Arise [from the depression and prostration in which circumstances have kept you—rise to a new life]! Shine (be radiant with the glory of the Lord), for your light has come, and the glory of the Lord has risen upon you! Isaiah 60:1

"Arise," according to *Strong's* (#6965), means "to get up, accomplish, continue, make good, ordain, stir up." God is calling us to arise out of our depression and the things that have prostrated us, kept us bent over and held us down. This is not the time to be controlled by our circumstances. It is not a time to

be oppressed or depressed. It is time to rise up to a new life.

In other words, God is saying, "Get up! It is time to accomplish the things that have been set before you. Continue on, don't stop! It is not the time to give up. Make good, turn things around and get rid of the things that are holding you back. Make things right. Stir up! Stir up the gifts that are within you, and allow yourself to be used by Me."

Shine—a Visible Glory

This word "shine," according to Strong's (#215), means "to be or make luminous (literally and metaphorically), break of day, glorious, kindle, be light, give light, set on fire, shine." Webster's synonyms for shine are "radiate, beam, sparkle, glare, coruscate, glitter and glisten." Coruscate means "flash, glitter, sparkle, gleam, radiate and shine." Sparkling, according to Webster's, implies "a shining intensely from radiant points or sparks by which the eye is dazzled." We are sparkling, glittering, gleaming and glistening, and there are radiant points or sparks that dazzle our eyes.

"Arise and shine," then, means to arise and sparkle, or glitter. This is incredible! We have read this scripture, taught it, prophesied it and declared it, but now, as the mysteries of the glory are being loosed in the earth, this verse takes on a whole new meaning. The very thing the Lord is pouring out upon us is clearly described in the Bible. God's people will be glittering in the earth.

The day the Lord showed this to me, I had just recently returned to Louisiana from attending Sister Ruth Ward Heflin's Ministers' Conference at her camp in Ashland, Virginia. From the time of my return, I had already ministered in five different meetings, and each of them was visited with manifestations of the presence of the Lord—gold dust and crystal. It was magnificent!

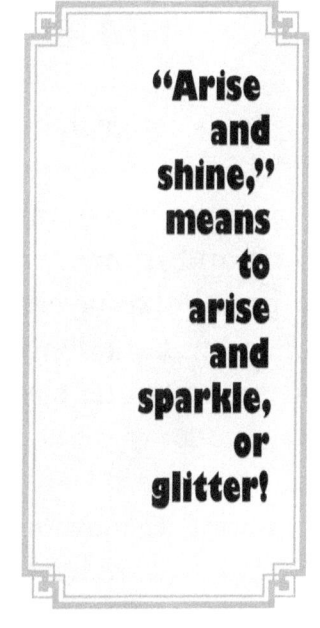

"Arise and shine," means to arise and sparkle, or glitter!

Look Up Isaiah 60

That particular morning, when I got up, I glanced in the mirror, and when I did, the Holy Spirit spoke to me to look up Isaiah 60. I opened the Bible and began to read, and this truth hit me immediately. I knew in an instant what the Lord was trying to say.

As I had been teaching these scriptures off and on through the years, I always realized that there was something more that we were not yet experiencing. When the revelation of the word *shine* came to me that morning, I suddenly knew what the Lord was trying to reveal to us.

It was late that evening before I had time to open some books and properly research the meanings of the words involved and come to a fuller understanding. Not surprisingly, everything I learned confirmed what the Lord had already spoken to me from Isaiah 60 that morning. God wants us to sparkle and glitter with His glory!

The Simplicity of the Revelation

I was astonished at the simplicity of this revelation. Why had I never seen it so clearly before? Revelation comes so easily in the glory, and we suddenly understand things we have previously struggled with. It seems like layers of a particular truth are pulled back, and suddenly we see more of it, and we see it with clarity and simplicity.

Suddenly we see the deeper meanings of a truth, much more profound than just the surface understanding we may have had for a while. At that point, the things that we have not understood or known become the new surface of our understanding, and we begin to build upon it. This all happens with great ease.

I was very excited about what I had learned, but I didn't have time to enjoy it. I had to get ready for the meeting that morning. I immediately left my books and went to the other room.

As I passed a mirror, I was amazed by what I saw. We had already seen some wonderful things in the glory in the days since stepping into this experience.

Gold dust was falling in our home as we worshiped the Lord or spoke of His glory. In each place where we sat to pray or worship, gold dust, diamond dust or crystal was being found covering the furniture. It was sticking to the wallpaper, and it was on our clothes in our closets and dressers.

But now, as I looked in the mirror, I saw something altogether new. A portion of my face around my right eye and my hair were covered with emerald flakes. Obedience to submit to the Spirit's promptings had further released His glory.

The feeling I had in that moment cannot be described. It was, at times, overwhelming. We had been permitted to step into a new and supernatural realm.

Some Meaningful Definitions

Webster's gives the following definitions:

Shine: "to gleam with illumination, light up; bring clarity, to be decorated with lights and color."

As we arise and shine, arising out of our depression and the circumstances that have held us prostrate, we begin to shine. As we shine, God is placing His glory upon us, and we are decorated with lights and color.

Sparkle: "a glowing particle, to glitter, to glisten as jewels, to give off sparks."

In this revival of the glory, we sparkle, we glitter and we glisten as jewels that give off sparks.

Glitter: "to shine, to sparkle with light, to glisten as a glittering sword."

As God's glory is being revealed in the earth, we shine and we sparkle with His light as glittering swords. So we are being illuminated, decorated with lights and color, and we glitter with glowing particles, as jewels, giving off sparks, shining, sparkling with lights and glistening as swords.

Shine Upon Us in Favor

Give ear, O Shepherd of Israel, You Who lead Joseph like a flock; You Who sit enthroned upon the cherubim [of the ark of the covenant], shine forth.
                                    Psalm 80:1

When God's face shines upon us, it will always be connected with His pleasure, His approval and His favor!

Restore us again, O God; and cause Your face to shine [in pleasure and approval on us] and we shall be saved!   Psalm 80:3

Arise and Shine

Restore us again, O God of hosts; and cause Your face to shine [upon us with favor as of old], and we shall be saved!   Psalm 80:7

Restore us, O Lord God of hosts; cause your face to shine [in pleasure, approval, and favor on us], and we shall be saved!   Psalm 80:19

When God's face shines upon us, it will always be connected with His pleasure, His approval and His favor. The Lord has always had set times to move, and this is His set time to favor Zion. Although we are always under the favor of God (as we maintain a right standing with Him), now the Lord is showing us that this is a specific time in which He will favor His people in specific ways:

Thou shalt arise, and have mercy upon Zion: for the time to favor her, yea, the set time, is come.   Psalm 102:13, KJV

A Set Time for Favor

On God's big heavenly clock, there are times set for Him to arise and favor His people. He is now shining upon His people, because the set time to favor us has come. The world will soon witness His favor upon us, and men and women will come to know that He is God. We have been favored in the past, but this present favor will go far beyond anything we have seen before. This supernatural favor will be visible to all.

The Glory of God Revealed

Webster's describes *favor* as "something to your advantage, to show partiality towards, to resemble in looks, the face, the countenance, an act of kindness going beyond what could normally be expected, an emblem or mark of support for some cause or individual, too great a kindness, kind indulgence, approval of, or having approval." In a set season of God's supernatural favor, things will suddenly be to your advantage. He will show supernatural partiality toward you.

You will also resemble Him in appearance. His face will become your face. His countenance will be upon you. He will perform supernatural acts of kindness for you that will go beyond what could normally be expected. There will be a divine mark of support upon you and upon your cause. So great a kindness will be your portion that everyone will know you have God's approval.

Webster's states: "the favorer is the one giving the favor, but especially the one that promotes or assists the success or prosperity of a cause or person." We are now in a season of God's set time to favor His people, and the One who is showing us this great favor is our "Favorer." He is promoting us and assisting us in the success and prosperity of our lives and ministries!

Job's Time for Favor

Job understood the favor of God:

That You would set a definite time and then re-member me earnestly [and imprint me on your heart]! If a man dies, shall he live again? All the days of my warfare and service I will wait, till my change and release shall come.

Job 14:13-14

Job knew that when times seemed worst for him, in the midst of his greatest distresses of life, the Lord would have a set time, an appointed time, and He would come and deliver him from all of his distresses and warfare. Because he understood God's set time to favor His children, he knew that his situation would change, and his release would come.

God had a set time to deliver the Israelites from bondage in Egypt, just as there was a set time for the Lamb of God to come to the earth to die for us, and there is a set time for the Lion of Judah to return. God has always had set, or designated, times. We are now in one of those preordained periods. This is a time God set long ago to favor us. He is shining upon us, and His glory is being seen, as His favor is being poured out.

This is the time. It is time for the world to see God's glory. It is time for the world to know that He is God. Very soon now, every knee will bow and every tongue will confess that He is Lord. That's why His light is arising upon us.

Isaiah foretold it:

For behold, darkness shall cover the earth, and dense darkness [all] peoples, but the Lord shall arise upon you ... , and His glory shall be seen on you. And nations shall come to your light, and kings to the brightness of your rising.

Isaiah 60:2-3

We are on the threshold of this, the greatest revival the world has ever seen, and in it, the nations will see the brightness of God's glory upon us. As a result, they will be drawn to the brightness of our rising. Even kings will come into this brightness.

In the Ministers' Conference in Ashland, Virginia, in January of 2000, someone stated that Smith Wigglesworth had prophesied about the last four great revivals that would come before the Lord's return. The first was the Charismatic Renewal. The second was the Word Movement. After that would come the Glory Revival, ushering in the last great harvest. At the end of that harvest, the Lord would return. Wigglesworth's young peers could not receive this prophetic word. They thought he must be getting too old and senile and that he did not know what he was talking about.

Many revivals have come and gone, and they have brought revelation, the power of God in demonstration and many changed lives. These came as a fulfillment of times the Lord set to release revival upon the earth. Now, we are in another of those set times, and God's favor is being outpoured upon the earth.

Anointed to Preach the Gospel

The Spirit of the Lord God is upon me, because the Lord has anointed and qualified me to preach the Gospel of good tidings to the meek, the poor, and afflicted; He has sent me to bind up and heal the brokenhearted, to proclaim liberty to the [physical and spiritual] captives and the opening of the prison and of the eyes to those who are bound, to proclaim the acceptable year of the Lord [the year of His favor] and the day of vengeance of our God, to comfort all who mourn. Isaiah 61:1-2

This same anointing now rests upon us, as we stand as the representatives of our Lord!

This passage, spoken prophetically by Isaiah, was again spoken hundreds of years later by the Lord Jesus Himself (see Luke 4:18). Isaiah therefore was speaking of the anointing that would rest upon the Savior of the world. It is this same anointing that now rests upon us, as we stand as the representatives of our Lord. He has granted us a power of attorney to operate in His stead.

79

This passage has been a *rhema* word to many of God's people. The passage speaks not only of the anointing for setting captives free, but it also speaks of Jubilee, the favor of the Lord. When Jesus stood in the synagogue that day, He stated, *"Today this Scripture has been fulfilled while you are present and hearing"* (Luke 4:21). He was not only declaring the anointing for setting the prisoners free, but also He was letting the world know that because He had come, the free favors of God would now profusely abound. He was our Grand Jubilee.

The anointing, the favor, Jubilee and Jesus (our Grand Jubilee) are all one. The free favors of God, His set time to favor, the anointing and Jubilee are all manifested to set captives free. Our Grand Jubilee came to set us free. He fulfilled the word of the Lord so that we might fulfill it too.

I am convinced that the visible glory of God that we are experiencing is a fulfillment of these prophecies of Isaiah. In recent times, the pages of our Bibles have sometimes been so highlighted with gold dust that we knew that what we were reading was directed by the Holy Spirit. He is the Spirit of knowledge and of revelation. What greater confirmation could there be to what we are reading than to have His visible seal of approval on it, a sprinkling of His glory? Since this phenomenon began, we have grown accustomed to having this beautiful golden glory covering not only our Bibles, but our clothes, our furniture and even our cars.

Sparks that Dazzle

Webster's not only describes *shine* as "sparkle and glitter," but also as "shining intensely from radiant points, or sparks, by which the eye is dazzled." This beautiful glory, in all of its many facets of color and appearance, not only sparkles and glitters, but it also sparks with radiant points that dazzle the eye. We see what looks like golden sparks shooting off of the faces of the people in our meetings. We have also seen what looks like golden sparks flying through the air as I am teaching the Word of God and sometimes even shooting off of the pages of the Bible as I am speaking from it. When this happens, it seems that tiny golden electrical charges are being released. There are so many of them at times that it is difficult for me to see the words on the page of the Bible well enough to continue reading.

God's glory is becoming visible to our eyes, and it is being seen by others around us. We need to be radiant with the glory of the Lord. To *be radiant* means "to shine brightly, to be lustrous, having luster, splendor, having the brilliance of the stars." That's what God wants for each of us.

Our Luminary Has Come

For your light has come.   Isaiah 60:1

Strong's (#216) states that this word *"light"* means "illumination or luminary (in every sense, including lightning, happiness, etc.): bright, clear, day, light, lightning, morning, sun." In other words, your illumination, or your luminary, has come.

A luminary is used to shed light in the midst of darkness. The One who shines upon you in the midst of gross darkness, the One who reflects Himself upon you, has come. Your happiness, your morning, has come. Arise! And shine!

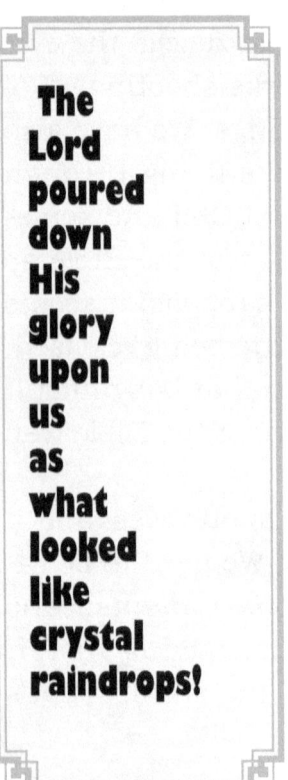

The Lord poured down His glory upon us as what looked like crystal raindrops!

And the glory of the Lord has risen upon you.
Isaiah 60:1

Yes, the glory has come upon you, and it can be seen upon you—not just metaphorically now, but literally.

The Spirit of Glory, the Spirit of God, is resting upon you.
1 Peter 4:14

More Visible Glory

From the time this manifestation began, it has been apparent in all of our gatherings. We were meeting in a Methodist church in Prairieville, Louisiana, loaned to us for our ministry. As we opened the praise and worship, speaking about the glory, people began to be covered with gold dust. As we proceeded with the meeting, praising and worshiping the Lord, it began to fall like rain—a visible golden rain.

People began to tell me that they were sitting in gold dust. It was all over the pulpit, the altar, the pews, my Bible, the floor and the people. And it also happened outside of the church too. It was suddenly in our cars, on our furniture and everywhere else we looked around us.

By the time of the next meeting in Prairieville a week later, the manifestations of the Lord's presence had intensified, and in our every meeting in other cities there was also an impartation of God's glory. It soon went beyond gold dust, to emerald, sapphire, ruby and crystal dust.

The following week, in the Methodist church, the Lord manifested all of these and more. Toward the end of the worship, the Lord poured down His glory upon us as what looked like crystal raindrops in the midst of the golden glory. This is the only way I know to describe what happened. These drops were everywhere, and we could not pick them up as fast as they fell.

This was not something that was seen and then disappeared. It was a tangible, clear, crystal-like substance that we could pick up and take with us. We decided that we would have it examined by a Christian jeweler friend, so we took some of these stones to his home. When he began to look at them, he couldn't believe what he was seeing, and he proceeded to tell us that the same substance had appeared in his home the night before we arrived. It happened as his children were worshiping the Lord. He had thought that the children had spilled some beads, and he swept them into a pile to be thrown into the trash.

As we talked about the manifestations of glory we were experiencing, the same crystal particles began to appear all around us again right there in his home. Our friend said they were pure crystal. Before we left that day, his whole family was covered in gold dust. He later examined the golden dust that appeared on his wife and children, and he said it was pure gold. As we were getting into our car to leave their home that day, the inside of our car was covered in gold dust, and crystals were beginning to appear on the floor.

A lady from another city in Louisiana was given one of the crystals that manifested in our meeting in the Methodist church, and she also took it to a jeweler to have it examined. That jeweler also said that it was pure crystal, and that if the pieces could be clustered together, they would form a topaz, either blue or gold.

That lady showed the crystal we gave her to everyone, testifying about God's glory being poured out in the earth, and as she was showing it for the Lord's glory, it changed color. Her jeweler then took it to be examined by another jeweler in Dallas, and when this man looked at it, he discovered it to be an alex-andrite, one of the rarest gems known to man (and worth about ten thousand dollars a carat).

Since that time, as we have been used to impart this glory into the lives of others, they, too, have be-gun to find stones of crystal and topaz, some clear and some golden, in their services and also in their homes.

These things are new to all of us, but Ezekiel saw such things in the Spirit when he was under a divine visitation and he saw the glory of the Lord, at the River Chebar. We, too, are seeing more and more of *The Glory of God Revealed.*

Father,

Help us to arise and shine and be radiant with Your glory. You are our Luminary, and You have come and are shining upon us. Shine upon us with Your favor and pleasure, and salvation will come. Your glory has risen upon us and can be visibly seen. Let Your light upon us draw the nations to our brightness and bring salvation to those who are in gross darkness.

Part II

Why the Glory?

Chapter 5

The Camels are Coming

Now Abraham was old, well advanced in years, and the Lord had blessed Abraham in all things. And Abraham said to the eldest servant of his house [Eliezer of Damascus], who ruled over all that he had, I beg of you, put your hand under my thigh; and you shall swear by the Lord, the God of heaven and earth, that you will not take a wife for my son from the daughters of the Canaanites, among whom I have settled. But you shall go to my country and to my relatives and take a wife for my son Isaac. Genesis 24:1-4

Abraham assigned his most trusted servant the responsibility of finding a wife for his son, Isaac. This servant, Eliezer, had ruled over Abraham's house and all that Abraham owned. Abraham told Eliezer to put his hand under his thigh and to swear by the Lord that he would not take, for his son Isaac, a wife from the daughters of the Canaanites. Isaac's bride would have to come from Abraham's own country. This act of Eliezer, placing his hand under Abraham's thigh and swearing by the Lord, was a sign of agreement to perform all that his master had required of him.

Although these scriptures speak to us of Abraham, Isaac, Eliezer and Rebekah, the beautiful bride found for Isaac, the story also presents us with many valuable types. Abraham, for example, is a type of the Father. Now He is sending forth the Holy Spirit into the earth to find a suitable Bride for His Son.

The Father is sending forth the Holy Spirit into the earth to find a suitable Bride for His Son!

The Meaning of the Names

The name *"Abraham,"* according to *Strong's* (#85), means "father of a multitude." Again, Abraham is a type of our heavenly Father, the Father of a multitude. The name *"Isaac," Strong's* (#3327), means "laughter," but his name also means "to take the right-hand side of." Isaac is a type of the Son, Jesus Christ, who took His rightful place, and is now seated at the right hand of His Father, God Almighty.

The name *"Eliezer,"* *Strong's* (#461), means "God of help." According to *Strong's* (#410), the first part of this name, *El* means "mighty, Almighty, deity, power" (it is the name of God), and the second part of the name, *ezer*, *Strong's* (#5828), means "aid, help." Therefore, the full name means "deity, mighty one, the one who aids, helper." Eliezer is a type of the Holy Spirit, and the Holy Spirit is God. He is the Mighty One who makes us mighty with His power. It is the Holy Spirit who comes to our aid and is our Helper in every time of need.

The name *"Rebekah,"* *Strong's* (#7259), means "to clog by tying up the fetlock, fettering (by beauty)." A *fetlock* is "a projection bearing a tuft of hair on the back of the leg above the hoof of a horse or similar animal."

To *clog* means "to add a weight to a man or an animal; to hinder motion; something that shackles or impedes movement." To clog the fetlock is "to place a weight, or shackle, around the tuft of hair above a horse's hoof to hinder its movement. Horses that drew carriages, after arriving at a particular destination, would be clogged by the driver. Weights would be placed around the fetlock to keep the horse stationary and to hinder any movement of the animal." To *fetter* is "to restrain from motion or action."

A Type of the Bride of Christ

Rebekah is a type of the Bride of Christ. When we become part of the Bride of Christ, our lives are no longer our own. We have been bought with a price. Because of the Lord's great love for us, He will, at times, clog us, in order to keep us from moving (except when He wants us to move) and to keep us standing still when He wants us to wait for His leading and direction. Paul wrote to the Corinthians:

For the love of Christ constraineth us.
2 Corinthians 5:14, KJV

The Amplified Bible renders this passage as:

For the love of God controls and urges and impels us.

In this way, our Lord becomes the Director of our lives. When we are married to the Lord, we are bound to Him with fetters of love. As we behold Him and we see His beauty and His magnificence, we are yoked to Him, fettered to Him, bound to Him, in love. When He beholds the beauty of His bride, He is restrained in His actions toward us. He withholds His wrath, is slow to anger and is also bound to us with fetters of love.

The Mission of Eliezer

Eliezer, a type of the Holy Spirit, was sent forth to find a wife for Isaac, a type of our Bridegroom, Jesus Christ. This bride could not be found among the Canaanites. In other words, the Bride of Christ cannot be of the world or of those who oppose the Kingdom of God; She must be part of God's Kingdom. She must have His blood flowing through her veins. She must be related to Him.

Eliezer, "the Holy Spirit," willingly accepted his charge:

And the servant took ten of his master's camels and departed, taking some of all his master's treasures with him. Genesis 24:10

Eliezer took ten camels with him, and the number ten speaks of reward or judgment. These camels were loaded down with his master's treasures. The King James Version says, *"... for all the goods of his master were in his hand."* The New Living Translation renders this phrase as: *" taking with him the best of everything his master owned."* This obviously speaks of the blessings and rewards of the Lord. These camels were loaded down with the treasures of the Kingdom, blessings and gifts, and, in the same way, the treasures of our Father's Kingdom are on their way to the Bride in these days. Everything that we

93

need in this hour for ministry is being released by the Holy Spirit.

Do you need a fresh anointing? It's on the way! Do you need the power of the Holy Spirit? It's on the way! Do you need finances? They're on the way. Oh, the camels are coming with everything you need!

Prophetic Insight

In December of 1999, I was on my way to minister in a meeting in the New Orleans area. God had been doing such amazing things in our meetings that we were in great anticipation of what He had in store for us next. We had prophetically stepped into the "new thing," not really knowing or understanding what it all meant. We just knew that the Lord was moving, and we wanted all that He had for us.

When I arrived at the meeting with several dear friends and intercessors, our hostess began to exclaim, "The camels are coming! The camels are coming! I don't know what it means. All I know is that the camels are coming!" I knew immediately that the Lord had spoken to her, and I knew that what the Lord had been showing me for months was real.

That night the Lord showed us that the camels that are coming are loaded down with goods from the Master's hands, and they are coming to bear gifts to His prospective Bride. I saw that these camels were not small, scrawny and weak animals. They were huge, powerful animals, massive in structure. And they were heavily loaded. In fact, they were overloaded with everything the Church, Christ's prospective Bride, needs for her success in all that is about to transpire in the earth.

The Camels Had Come Before

I find it interesting that Jesus, after His birth, was visited by wise men riding camels loaded down with precious gifts. Those camels had come a great distance and were carrying a precious cargo. Among the gifts they carried were gold, frankincense and myrrh.

The word *"gold," Strong's* (#5557), means "(through the idea of the utility of the metal) gold; a golden article, as an ornament or coin, ... from the base of #5530," meaning "to furnish what is needed; to graze [touch slightly], light upon, to employ or to act towards one in a given manner: entreat, use." Just as that precious gold was brought

Just as precious gold was brought to the Redeemer of the world by camels that were loaded down, gold has now come to us!

to the Redeemer of the world by camels that were loaded down, gold has now come to us.

The baby Jesus was God revealed in the flesh, the Christ, the Anointed One, in the form of an infant, and the gold brought to Him signified that He was fully furnished with all that was needed to accomplish His great commission, the redemption of all humanity. He had the touch of Heaven upon Him, and He was grazed by the markings of His Father. He was lit upon and employed by the Father. His Father was acting toward him with favor because he would now be used and directed by God's hand.

They're Coming Again

I see the camels coming to God's people, and they are loaded down with many different things—not just gold. This signifies to me that God's Church is being fully furnished with all that is needed to accomplish the Great Commission left to us to bring in a great harvest of souls.

The Father has grazed us. We are marked by Him and for Him. It only takes the slightest touch from Him, and we are transformed into all that He has called us to be. He has employed us to be laborers in His great vineyard. He is acting towards us in His grace, mercy and favor. He is entreating us to be used in His Kingdom.

The word *"myrrh," Strong's* (#4666), means "strengthened for," *Strong's* (#4753), "an armament, a body of troops; army, soldier, man of war," and *Strong's* (#4754), "to serve in a military campaign; to execute the apostolate, to contend with carnal inclinations: soldier, (go to) war."

This word *armament* means "military equipment, a military force, means of protection or defense, armor, the process of being prepared for war." *Apostolate* means "the office of an apostle." Therefore, to "execute the apostolate" is to execute the office of an apostle.

Jesus is our Man of War:

Who is the King of glory? The Lord strong and mighty, the Lord mighty in battle.
Who is [He then] this King of glory? The Lord of hosts, He is the King of glory.

Psalm 24:8 and 10

Jesus is the Captain of the Hosts, the Chief Executive Officer of the armies of Heaven. He is the Lord of the battle. He is our armor, our defense. He is the One who establishes and executes the heavenly apostolate.

We are His body of troops, and we are becoming a great army that will move through the earth, bringing salvation, gathering in the harvest and flowing in signs and wonders to demonstrate to the earth that there is a true and living God. We are soldiers enlisted in the greatest military campaign. We are His military equipment, a great military force, and we are in the process of being prepared for war. There is coming a great execution of the apostolic in the earth.

The word *"frankincense," Strong's* (#3030), means "incense tree, or incense itself." In the Scriptures, incense always speaks of intercession, or prayer. Jesus became our Great Intercessor, and He has imparted to us the power of prayer and intercession.

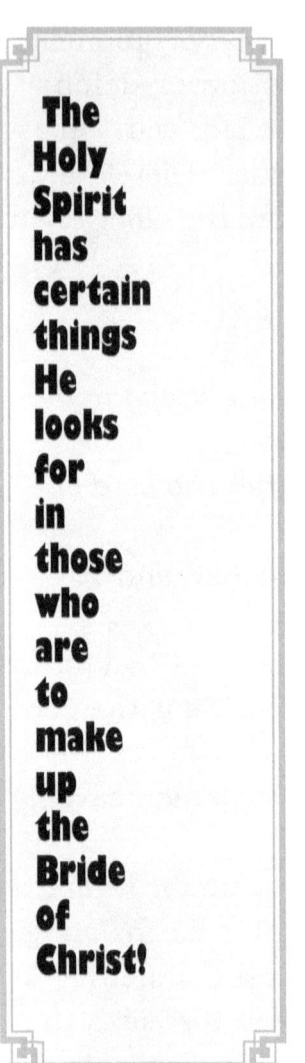

The Holy Spirit has certain things He looks for in those who are to make up the Bride of Christ!

The camels that came to visit the young child Jesus were loaded down with gold, frankincense and myrrh, and the camels are now coming again, bringing to the Lord's Church all that is needed for her equipping in this hour.

The gold dust or the sprinkling of other colors that is coming into our meetings is not an end in itself. It is God's visible, manifested glory, and when it is revealed, it is just a glimpse of many greater things to come. It is a symbol of God's power. He is preparing to do far greater things through His Body, His Church, His prospective Bride.

At the Time When Women Go Out to Draw Water

And he made his camels to kneel down outside the city by a well of water at the time of the evening when women go out to draw water.
See, I stand here by the well of water, and the daughters of the men of the city are coming to draw water. Genesis 24:11 and 13

It was a very strategic time for Eliezer to arrive at the well. In the evening hours, all of the young women of the area came to the well to draw water, and the young men came also to search out a prospective bride. Since this was Eliezer's mission, he was in the right place at the right time.

Again, this is the mission of the Holy Spirit in this hour. He is at the wells of salvation, searching for a prospective Bride for Christ from among those who are drawing water from the wells of His Kingdom. He is just on time. Let us go out to draw water.

She Must Receive My Camels

And let it so be that the girl to whom I say, I pray you, let down your jar that I may drink, and she replies, Drink, and I will give your camels drink also—let her be the one whom You have selected and appointed and indicated for Your servant Isaac [to be a wife to him]; and by it I shall know

that You have shown kindness and faithfulness
to my master. Genesis 24:14

Eliezer set some strict qualifications for the bride-to-be for Isaac, and the most strict of those was the lineage from which she must come. And just as Rebekah had to be from the right lineage, we, as the Bride of Christ, must be of His lineage. Rebekah had to be kinfolk, family, and so do we. This is the most important thing the Holy Spirit looks for as He searches for those who are to make up the Bride of Christ.

But not only was the Bride of Isaac to be of the proper lineage, to be beautiful to behold and to be a woman of modesty, she would also have to meet Eliezer's requirements in regard to watering his camels. It was not enough for her just to receive and welcome him; she would have to offer to water his camels as well. This would reveal whether or not she possessed the all-important heart of a servant.

The camels were important, for they bore the load of gifts, and Isaac's bride must recognize this. If she was to receive the gifts sent to her, she must value them. God's great gifts will be given only to those who appreciate them. Although every provision is being made for the Kingdom, these provisions will be given only to those who welcome them and realize their worth. All of the goods from the Master's hands, all the treasures of His Kingdom, the very best He has, is being loosed for God's people, but we must be willing and eager to receive it.

Rebekah would pass the test. She met the requirements set by Eliezer (the Holy Spirit). So now it was fully proper for the engagement to take place.

The Engagement Takes Place

And when the camels had finished drinking, the man took a gold earring or nose ring of half a shekel in weight, and for her hands two bracelets of ten shekels in weight in gold.

Genesis 24:22

When the engagement process begins with a young Jewish couple, the prospective groom gives jewelry to his bride-to-be. This marks her as his. Then all the other young men of the village know that this young lady is already spoken for, and it is "hands off" for them. It is the same when we are beginning the engagement process with our King of Glory. He is marking us as His own, and once we are marked by God, it is "hands off" for the enemy of our soul. In another chapter, we will see the meaning of some of the jewelry that He is placing upon us, as we become marked as His.

Making Room for the Holy Spirit

And [Eliezer] said, Whose daughter are you? I pray you tell me: Is there room in your father's house for us to lodge there?   Genesis 24:23

Is there room for the Holy Spirit in your life? When a time of visitation from the Holy Spirit comes, we must always make room for it.

When Laban, Rebekah's brother, was made aware of what was transpiring with his sister, he ran to the well to meet Eliezer and Rebekah:

He cried, Come in, you blessed of the Lord! ... For I have made the house ready and have prepared a place for the camels. Genesis 24:31

Laban also welcomed the Holy Spirit and made room for Him. He prepared his house for this great visitation. He made room for his great guest, cleaning things up in preparation for His coming.

This is very exciting. Not only did Rebekah received Eliezer (the type of the Holy Spirit), but her entire household welcomed him. And by welcoming Eliezer, they were welcoming a move of God. There was no hesitation on their part, and this opened them to a higher level of blessing, simply because they were so willing to embrace the Holy Spirit and His work.

A Season of Preparation

We are now in a season of great preparation, and a part of that preparation is getting things cleaned up and in proper order so that when the Holy Spirit is ready for a great visitation, we can say, "Holy Spirit, come on in! We're ready for You!" There must be no hesitation on our part. We must be so ready and willing for the Spirit to come that we run after Him and the things He is doing in the earth.

Not only did Laban make room for Eliezer; he also made room for Eliezer's camels. Many times our capacity for God is much too small, so small that it leaves no room for the Holy Spirit to move. The Lord wants to give to us more then we can imagine, but too many of us have boxed Him in. Our concept of the Lord is entirely too small. He wants to bless us with greater anointing, more power and more of the gifts, but we must enlarge our capacity for Him so that we can receive all that He has for us.

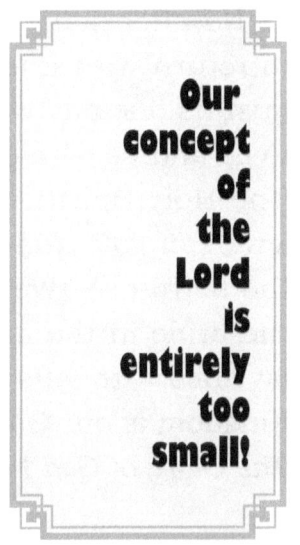

Our concept of the Lord is entirely too small!

The Holy Spirit is presenting Himself to us, and if we can receive Him, embracing and welcoming His arrival, we will soon see a corresponding release of all the provision needed.

Jewels of Silver and Gold

Rebekah is before you; take her and go, and let her be the wife of your master's son, as the Lord has said. And when Abraham's servant heard their words, he bowed himself to the ground be-fore the Lord. And the servant brought out jewels of silver, jewels of gold, and garments and gave them to Rebekah; he also gave precious things to her brother and her mother.

Genesis 24:51-53

Now Rebekah, the prospective bride, was released to return with Eliezer to become the bride of Isaac (just as one day we will be released from this earth to go and be with our Heavenly Bridegroom). Eliezer (the Holy Spirit), then gave the prospective bride jewels of gold and silver as part of the finalizing of the betrothal. (We will see more on the dressing of the bride in the next chapter.) Today we are being lavished with gifts in recognition of our place in the Kingdom of our God. The result is that we are seeing *The Glory of God Revealed.*

Father,

Everything we need in this hour is available to us. All the goods of the Kingdom are being released for our success. Help us to make room for You and for all You want to do in our lives.

Chapter 6

Dressing the Bride

And say, Thus says the Lord God to Jerusalem [representing Israel]: Your [spiritual] origin and your birth are thoroughly Canaanitish; your [spiritual] father was an Amorite and your [spiritual] mother a Hittite. And as for your birth, on the day you were born your navel cord was not cut, nor were you washed with water to cleanse you, nor rubbed with salt or swaddled with bands at all. Ezekiel 16:3-4

Part of the finalizing of the Jewish betrothal is the dressing and adorning of the bride. She is dressed in beautiful garments and arrayed with gold and silver. The bridegroom takes great pride in providing the very best for her. This is taking place with us right now, as the Lord's glory is being released in the earth. He is dressing His Bride, clothing us in magnificence. He is decking us in gold and silver and many precious jewels, with dustings of emeralds, rubies, sapphires, diamonds and crystal.

In this chapter of Ezekiel, we see a developing relationship between the Lord of glory and Israel, His prospective Bride. This is also a type of our relationship with the Lord, our heavenly Bridegroom. Ours is a growing relationship too, a progressive work.

Even though, in this scripture, the Lord is speaking of Israel, what He says is equally true of us. This, then, is a parallel of our own beginnings, from the point of salvation, where the Lord found us, to the place He is currently bringing us to.

The Lord began verse 3 by reminding Israel of just where she had come from. Her origins, the Lord showed her, were totally Canaanitish. Her father was an Amorite, and her mother a Hittite. In other words, these people were descended from a family of idolaters. The Canaanites and the Amorites were unclean and stood for everything that was against God. They were His enemies.

The same can be said of us. Until Christ found us and bought us back, we were of the Adamic nature. We were totally Canaanitish. Thank God that He took pity upon us:

No eye pitied you to do any of these things for you, to have compassion on you; but you were cast out in the open field, for your person was abhorrent and loathsome on the day that you were born. And when I passed by you and saw you rolling about in your blood, I said to you in your blood, Live! Yes, I said to you still in your natal blood, Live! Ezekiel 16:5-6

Throughout all of eternity we will be thankful to God that when He passed by us, and we were dying in our own trespasses and sins, He spoke to us, "Live!"

Beginning to Mature

I caused you [Israel] to multiply as the bud which grows in the field, and you increased and became tall and you came to full maidenhood and beauty; your breasts were formed and your hair had grown, yet you were naked and bare. Ezekiel 16:7

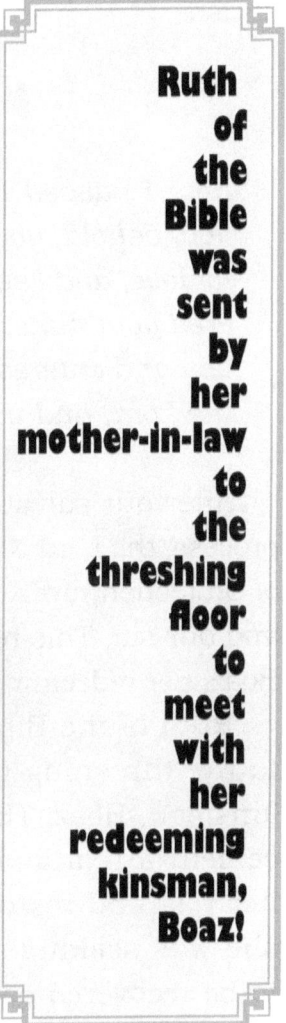

Ruth of the Bible was sent by her mother-in-law to the threshing floor to meet with her redeeming kinsman, Boaz!

"Your breasts were formed" speaks of maturing, so God was saying to Israel, "You were beginning to grow up and mature." *"You hair had*

grown" simply means that Israel was becoming consecrated, set apart. Yet she was still uncovered, *"naked,"* just as we were in the beginning stages of our salvation and the redemptive work of the cross in us.

At the Time for Love

Now I passed by you again and looked upon you; behold, you were maturing and at the time for love, and I spread My skirt over you and covered your nakedness. Yes, I plighted My troth to you and entered into a covenant with you, says the Lord, and you became Mine. Ezekiel 16:8

After our salvation, as we begin to mature, in the process, the Lord comes and spreads His skirt, His wing of protection, over us. He, thus, covers our nakedness and our sin. This reminds me of the story of Ruth and Boaz, her redeeming kinsman (a type of Christ).

Ruth of the Bible was sent by her mother-in-law to the threshing floor to meet with her redeeming kinsman, Boaz. The purpose in Ruth's going was to cement a relationship with Boaz that would bring her rest and restore her inheritance. The rest that she was seeking and the inheritance that needed to be recovered could only come about through her marriage to the redeeming kinsman.

Boaz, again, was a type of the Christ, our Redeeming Kinsman. It is only through our relationship with

Him, our Husband, that we can find rest and the restoration of all things to our lives.

It was not until Ruth went to the threshing floor to lie at the feet of Boaz that he could spread his protection over her. The fact that he took the edge of his skirt and spread it over her signified that there would be a wedding. This was his way of proposing marriage. Ruth was ready for Boaz's love and welcomed his proposal.

You were maturing and at the time [ready] for
love.   Ezekiel 16:8

We have not always been ready for God's love. When we are ready to love and be loved, the Lord is ready to spread His skirt over us and cover our nakedness.

There is a cry going forth today to the Bridegroom, an intercession that ascends to His throne. It is an expression of our passion for Him, this cry, this call, this expression of our desire. It is the sound of love for the One whom our hearts desire.

The Lord knows when His Bride is ready for Him, and He spreads the borders of His garment to cover us. He extends over us His wing of protection. This signifies that the wedding is as good as done. He is now spreading His canopy of glory over us:

For over all the glory shall be a canopy (a defense
of divine love and protection).   Isaiah 4:5

God's glory is upon His Bride, and wherever she is, that glory will be seen. His glory becomes a covering, a canopy that hides, defends and protects us in His divine love.

First, however, must come the cleansing, and only then can the dressing begin:

Now again, the Lord is dressing His Bride and marking her as His own!

Then I washed you with water; yes, I thoroughly washed away your [clinging] blood from you and I anointed you with oil.   Ezekiel 16:9

The Dressing Begins

I clothed you also with embroidered cloth and shod you with [fine seal] leather; and I girded you about with fine linen and covered you with silk.   Ezekiel 16:10

This is the beginning of the dressing process for the Bride, and verses 10 to 13 go on to present a prophetic representation of just how the Lord will prepare her. Here we see our relationship with our Bridegroom, our total dependence upon Him. He is the Authority and Source for our lives, and He is calling for our complete surrender to His will for our lives.

As the Lord speaks of dressing His Bride to be, He tells her that He has already dressed her in the past, but even though He dressed her as His Bride and marked her as His own, she fell into sin, into idolatry, and had to be stripped of all that He had done for her. Now, again, the Lord is dressing His Bride and marking her as His own. He is putting upon her signs of the engagement.

A Double Embroidered Work

I clothed you also with embroidered cloth.
                                    Ezekiel 16:10

This word *"clothe,"* according to *Strong's* (#3847), means "to wrap around, to put on a garment or clothe oneself or another, literally or figuratively: (in) apparel, arm, array (self), clothe (self), come upon, put (on, upon), wear." *Embroidered work*, according to *Strong's* (#7553), means "variegation of color, divers colors, raiment of needlework on both sides," and according to *Strong's* (#7551), "to variegate color, to fabricate, curiously work." For the Lord to dress us simply means that He clothes us, wraps His garments around us, comes upon us, arms us and arrays us.

We are *"arrayed,"* which means "to be dressed magnificently." Psalm 29:2 tells us to worship the Lord *"in the beauty of holiness or in holy array."* As we worship the Lord, we are being dressed magnificently by Him. It is He that is coming upon us, wrapping around us, arming us and arraying us.

As the Lord dresses us magnificently in His embroidered work, it is in a variegation, a variety, of colors. His is an embroidered work that is quite varied and diverse in its workmanship.

This is also a dual workmanship. Not only is it embroidered on the outside; it is also embroidered on the inside. It is a double-sided piece of embroidery.

The embroidery on the outside is to be seen, but there is more on the inside. In the same way, the work the Lord does in our lives is not just an outward work. The inward work that He does is much more important.

A regular piece of embroidery work is very beautiful and intricate on the outside. However, the underside, which is not designed to be seen, is nothing special to behold. In fact, it is a conglomeration of threads that has no attraction at all. The work the Lord is doing in us is a double embroidered work. It is beautiful within and without, equally attractive on both sides. What He is embroidering inside of us is equally as beautiful as the picture being formed on the outside.

The colors spoken of in this passage are royal in appearance. They are the colors of the priesthood, the royal colors used in the Tabernacle of God's presence. The beautifully colored stones that were on the breastplate of the high priest represented the twelve tribes of Israel, God's people. The gold and silver represented His deity and redemption, and the red stood for the cleansing power of His blood to be shed.

Every one of these colors represented you and me, for we are a royal priesthood. We are God's Tabernacle. We are the beautiful stones that lay next to His breast. We are His people. His redemptive work at Calvary has set us free. All that He is, He works into our lives, and we become what He is.

A Protective Covering

I shod you with [fine seal] leather.

Ezekiel 16:10

The King James Version translates this phrase *"fine seal leather"* as *"badgers' skin."* *"Shod,"* according to *Strong's* (#5274), means "to fasten up, to sandal, to furnish with sandals, to bolt, lock, shut up." The giving of sandals was a sign of covenant. Also a slipper or sandal was a symbol of occupancy or of marriage. Not only are we in covenant with the King of Glory, but He has taken up occupancy with us, and we with Him. He is our Husband, the One we are betrothed to and the One with whom we abide in covenant.

"No Sweat"

And I girded you about with fine linen.

Ezekiel 16:10

We are in a season of rest. Not only have we entered into what is commonly being called "the third day," but we have also entered into the seventh day—a Sabbath-rest. We will, no doubt, work harder for the Lord in the days ahead and accomplish more, but it will be the Lord doing the work through us. All the things that God's people have striven to accomplish in the past will now be brought about with ease by the Spirit of the Lord, because this is an hour of rest. He will just do it.

Linen speaks of the rest of God, and being dressed in linen speaks of no human effort, or "no sweat" on our part. A season of rest speaks of God doing the work, with no human effort involved.

When they enter the gates of the inner court, they shall be clothed in linen garments; no wool shall be on them while they minister at the gates of the inner court and within the temple. They shall have linen turbans on their heads and linen breeches upon their loins; they shall not gird themselves with anything that causes [them to] sweat.   Ezekiel 44:17-18

When the priests of the Old Testament went into the Inner Court, or the Holy of Holies, they could wear only linen. There could be no perspiration allowed in the Holy of Holies. In other words, no human effort could exist there. No perspiration, no sweat, could be involved in the holy things of God. A season of rest means a "no sweat" situation, and this is what God is doing for us.

Something Much Deeper

There is something much deeper to be seen in this passage. The heads of the priests and their loins also had to be covered with linen. This speaks of a mind-set. It was not just their bodies that had to be covered with a fabric that would not produce perspiration. The Lord is calling us, as His New Testament priests, to have a "no sweat" mentality. He wants to embed into our thinking the fact that things will not happen because of human effort. They will happen only if He is doing the work.

We must choose to enter into the rest that God has prepared for us. Because Israel could not believe Him, trust Him, rely on Him and cling to Him, He swore in His wrath that they would not enter into His rest:

Because of the disobedience of Moses in this situation, he was not allowed to enter the Promised Land!

117

For in a certain place He has said this about the seventh day: And God rested on the seventh day from all His works. And [they forfeited their part in it, for] in this [passage] He said, They shall not enter My rest.   Hebrews 4:4-5
(see also Genesis 2:2)

It was always God's plan for His people to enter into His rest. Hebrews, in fact, goes on to tell us that the people of Israel had formerly been given the good news about entering into God's rest, but they failed to appropriate it and did not enter because of disobedience:

Seeing then that the promise remains over [from past times] for some to enter that rest, and that those who formerly were given the good news about it and the opportunity, failed to appropriate it and did not enter because of disobedience, again He sets a definite day, [a new] Today, [and gives another opportunity of securing that rest] saying through David after so long a time in the words already quoted, Today, if you would hear His voice and when you hear it, do not harden your hearts.   Hebrews 4:6-7

This promise of rest was not only for the Hebrews of one generation. The promise continued in effect for all those who would appropriate it in generations to come. Today, not only is that same provision still available to us, but we are a third day bride that has entered the seventh day, the Day of Rest. Now, as never before, God's rest is available to us.

The Lord makes it very easy for us and all we have to do is hear His voice and not allow our hearts to be hardened as those of the Israelites in the day of provocation.

A Day of Provocation

Psalm 95:7-9 speaks of a day of provocation, when God's people tried, tested, proved and provoked the Lord to judgment. Exodus 17:1-7 speaks of the Lord bringing Israel to the wilderness of Rephidim, where there was no water. There the Lord provided a rock for Moses to strike, and water came out of it to meet the need of the entire nation. But because the people tempted and tried the patience of the Lord—asking "Is the Lord among us or not?"—He changed the name of Rephidim to Massah and Meribah, meaning "proof" and "contention."

God would then take them back again to Rephidim, and this time the Lord would tell Moses to simply speak to the rock to get water. The New Testament also speaks of this rock in the desert out of which the water gushed, and tells us that it *"was Christ."* Moses was to speak to the rock and not strike it, for the Rock, which is Christ, has already been smitten—at Calvary—once and for all.

Whenever we have unbelief about the things of God or about God meeting our needs, we are striking the Rock. All we have to do is to speak to the Rock. He hears us and answers us. Because of the disobedience of Moses in this situation, he was not allowed to enter the Promised Land, and the people who had heard the good news of entering the rest of God would thus forfeit their rights.

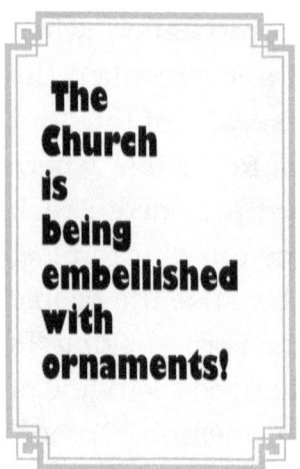

The Church is being embellished with ornaments!

[This mention of a rest was not a reference to their entering into Canaan.] For if Joshua had given them rest, He [God] would not speak afterward about another day. So then, there is still awaiting a full and complete Sabbath-rest reserved for the [true] people of God; for he who has once entered [God's] rest also has ceased from [the weariness and pain] of human labors, just as God rested from those labors peculiarly His own. Let us therefore be zealous and exert ourselves and strive diligently to enter that rest [of God, to know and experience it for ourselves], that no one may fall or perish by the same kind of unbelief and disobedience [into which those in the wilderness fell].

Hebrews 4:8-11

It is interesting, because when the Lord speaks of dressing Israel, as He is now doing with us, the Bible actually says that He girded her in fine linen, as in *"gird up the loins of your mind"* (1 Peter 1:13, KJV)." *"Gird,"* according to *Strong's* (#2280), means "to wrap firmly (especially a turban, compress, or saddle); to stop, to rule: govern, healer." This again speaks of the girding of the mind. Once our minds are girded in linen, our mind-sets become no-human-effort mind-sets. Then the Lord can more freely govern us, saddle us, rule us, stop us from going in the wrong direction and heal us.

This is the hour of rest, a "no-sweat" time for those who are His, so God is dressing His Bride in fine linen.

Pulled Out of Your Cocoon

And I covered you with silk. Ezekiel 16:10

Strong's (#3680 and #3780) reveals that the word *"cover"* means "to plump up, to cover in clothing or secrecy, fill up hollows." The Lord covers us with silk, as in clothing. I also believe that this speaks of the anointing—to be plumped up, made fat, with the anointing. *To fill up the hollows* speaks of the empty places, the voided places, the hollow places in our lives being filled with the anointing. *To cover in secrecy* speaks of divine protection from the enemy.

The Father is covering us with silk. *Strong's* (#4897 and #4871) reveals that the word *"silk"* simply means "as drawn from the cocoon" or "draw out." As the Lord is dressing His Bride in silk and anointing her, as He covers her and His divine protection is upon her, He is drawing her out of her cocoon, to be used and to be displayed in the earth.

Much of the Bride, at this very moment, is hidden, concealed from the world and even from much of the rest of the Church. I believe that as the Bride is being dressed in silk, she is also being pulled out of her obscurity and hiding, to be presented as the Lord's approved.

Embellishments

I decked you also with ornaments and I put bracelets on your wrists and a chain on your neck. Ezekiel 16:11

This word *decked* simply means "to cover, clothe with elegance, to embellish." An *ornament* is "a person whose character or talents adds luster to his surroundings or society." The Church is being embellished with ornaments, persons whose character and talents add luster to their surroundings and society. Those whose character and talents add luster, brightness, splendor and brilliancy will be added to us. If we are the Bride of Christ, then our ministries will be dressed and embellished with beautiful ornaments, persons with excellent character and talents who will add to all that we do.

Linked to Him

I put bracelets upon thy hands.

Ezekiel 16:11, KJV

"Bracelet," according to *Strong's* (#6781 and #6775), means "to be linked to, to serve, (mentally) contrive." *"Hand," Strong's* (#3027), speaks of "a hand (the open one [indicating power, means, direction]; dominion, fellowship, ministry." We are linked to our Lord, and we serve Him—spiritually and mentally.

This is not a head issue. It's just a fact that we know. We serve Him, and we are linked to Him. He is our Source. It is only through being linked with Him that we have any dominion in the Kingdom and any true fellowship—with the Lord and with His saints. As we serve and are linked to Him, only then can we have open hands. Only then are we given power, and the means that we need can flow to us. Only then can direction come, and the flow of ministry take place.

He Is Our Authority

A chain upon your neck ...   Ezekiel 16:11

"Chain," Strong's (#7242), speaks of "a binding together, to confine, fetters of slavery, linked together,

to unite closely, and strongly attached." The *"neck,"* *Strong's* (#1627), speaks of "the place of authority." In Bible days, when any king was victorious over another king in battle, the victorious king would put his foot upon the neck of his defeated foe. This signified that the victorious king was destroying the authority of his enemy.

Our place of authority comes only as we are bound together with the Lord. It is as we are linked to Him, and only to Him, that His authority becomes our authority. We have no authority except through our submission to Christ and those whom Christ has placed over us. We are confined to Him, with fetters of slavery, and we are strongly attached to Him and to His Word.

Paul identified himself as a bondservant to Christ. He was marked as a servant of the Lord, marked in such a way that it was as if his ear had been driven through with an awl. He was pierced and marked for life—a slave by choice.

Prepared

And I put a ring on your nostril and earrings in your ears and a beautiful crown upon your head!
Ezekiel 16:12

This phrase *"a ring in your nostril"* is translated in the King James Version of the Bible as *"a jewel on thy forehead."* This word *"jewel," Strong's* (#3627), means "something prepared (as an implement, uten-sil, dress): armour, artillery." *"Forehead,"* Strong's (#639), means "the nose or nostril, face, person (from the rapid breathing in passion) countenance, forbearing, long-suffering, worthy." When God sends us jewels, it means that we are being prepared for the marriage. His work in us is being completed. This is also a sign of our armor and of our artillery.

The fact that we are cur-rently being decorated with various colors and with jewels, such as emeralds, sapphires, rubies and others, comes as a result of rapid breathing in passion, as we worship our Lord. The Bride is experiencing a new passion for her Lord and God and King. This is happen-ing now as at no other time in history. And our Lord also has a passion for us.

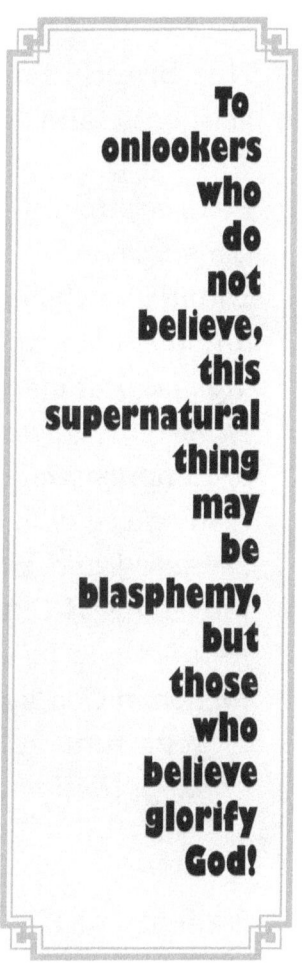

To onlookers who do not believe, this supernatural thing may be blasphemy, but those who believe glorify God!

As we praise and worship the Lord in passion, the glory comes. Through an expression of our passion for Him and His passion for us, the realms of glory are released upon us, realms of the supernatural. Then the heavens are opened, and the jewels of Heaven are placed upon us.

A Fiery Ordeal

This beautiful decking also comes as a result of longsuffering and forbearance:

Beloved, do not be amazed and bewildered at the fiery ordeal which is taking place to test your quality, as though something strange (unusual and alien to you and your position) were befalling you. But insofar as you are sharing Christ's sufferings, rejoice, so that when His glory [full of radiance and splendor] is revealed, you may also rejoice with triumph [exultantly]. If you are censured and suffer abuse [because you bear] the name of Christ, blessed [are you—happy, fortunate, to be envied, with life-joy, and satisfaction in God's favor and salvation, regardless of your outward condition], because the Spirit of glory, the Spirit of God, is resting upon you.

1 Peter 4:12-14

Hallelujah! If you are suffering for the sake of Christ, when the glory is revealed, full of splendor and radiance, you will rejoice, because the Spirit of glory, which is the Spirit of God, will rest upon you. You will be dressed and clothed magnificently in the glory. It is even now being manifested in many forms.

Not everyone will believe, even when they see it:
*On their part He is blasphemed, but on your part
He is glorified.* 1 Peter 4:14

To those onlookers who do not understand or
believe that this supernatural thing is of the Lord,
it may indeed be blasphemy, but those who believe
glorify God.

Ears to Hear

And earrings in your ears ... Ezekiel 16:12

The Lord marks us with earrings, signifying that
He gives us *"ears to hear."*

In this hour, as never before, we must be able
to hear the things of the Spirit, even as the Lord is
dressing His Bride and equipping her for this hour.
The full provision is given to keep us from the voices
around us, the voice of the enemy and the voices of
the world.

Protection

And a beautiful crown upon your head!
Ezekiel 16:12

This word *"crown," Strong's* (#5899 from #5849),
means "to encircle for attack or protection." This
word *"head," Strong's* (#7218), means "the head

(as most easily shaken): chiefest place, highest part." God places on us a crown of protection from all attacks at the most easily shaken part of the body, the head.

Decking the Bride

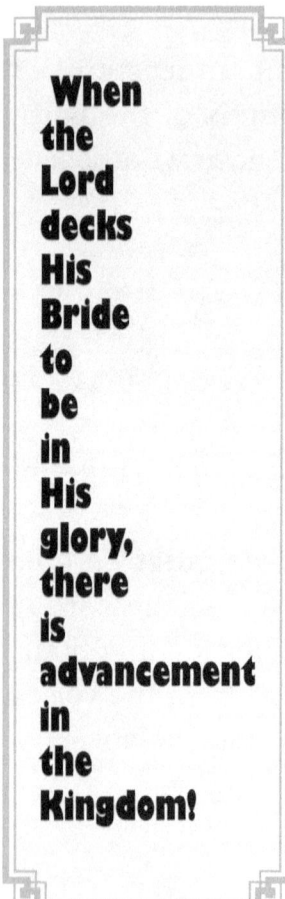

When the Lord decks His Bride to be in His glory, there is advancement in the Kingdom!

Thus you were decked with gold and silver, and your raiment was of fine linen and silk and embroidered cloth; you ate fine flour and honey and oil. And you were exceedingly beautiful and you prospered into royal estate.

Ezekiel 16:13

This word *"decked," Strong's* (#5710), means "to advance, i.e., pass on or continue; bring to put an ornament upon, adorn, pass by." When the Lord decks His Bride to be in His glory, there is advancement in the Kingdom. We pass on to the next phase of destiny. We are able to move up higher in Him.

An ornament is placed upon us. We are adorned, and I believe that in this decking, the Lord has passed by us and equipped us to also pass by the obstacles that have hindered us and halted us in the past. God is ornamenting us *"with gold and silver."*

"Gold," Strong's (#2091), means "to shimmer; something gold-colored (i.e., yellow), as oil." Gold also represents the deity of our Lord. Many ask, "Is this really gold?" Well, we had a jeweler examine the gold flecks he saw on his wife's face, and he found them to be pure gold.

Golden oil also manifests in our meetings. Many times when the gold dust and other shimmering particles have appeared, puddles of golden oil have also appeared on church pews, and as I have preached many of those in the congregation have begun to have a golden oil forming in the palms of their hands.

"Silver," Strong's (#3701), means "money, redemption." One of our intercessors has had silver dust appear in many parts of her home during times of intercession. Many other prayer warriors, as they have answered the call to intercede for others, have experienced silver dust appearing all over them.

We have found that this dusting of God's glory upon His people is a very powerful tool that touches people's lives and brings them into the Kingdom. As the dusting of His glory comes upon us, it is to be a sign to the unbeliever of God's magnificent power and His love toward them.

As Jesus betroths His Bride to Himself, He dresses her, He decks her and He feeds her with the finest oil and honey. She is made to prosper *"into royal estate."*

When the children of Israel were being delivered from Egypt, the Lord told them that if they would remain faithful to Him through the wilderness He would make them a kingdom of priests and would bring them into a royal estate. At the moment they were coming out of Egypt, they didn't look much like a kingdom of priests. Yet, forty years later, as they were marching in to possess their Promised Land, it became apparent that God had kept His promise. His people were entering as royalty, a kingdom of priests. They had come forth from Egypt and its from slavery and bondage, but were now being brought into the land as heirs of the Kingdom, a people of royalty, children of the King.

As they marched into the land that day, the priests carried the Ark of the Covenant before the people, while the forty thousand among them who were dressed for war crossed over the Jordan River. They looked very different that day than when they had come out of Egypt.

It is the same for us today. The Lord finds us lost and dying in our sins. He speaks to us, "Live," and we begin to live. Then, He begins to clothe and adorn us.

We have stayed with Him through the wilderness, and now He is bringing us into the land to possess all that He has for us. As a sign of that, He is decking us, His potential Bride, with gold and silver. This is *The Glory of God Revealed.*

Dear Jesus,

You have called us out of darkness into Your marvelous light. You have delivered us out of the grasp of Egypt, and You want to bring us into all of the things You have promised us. In this hour, You are dressing us, and You are bringing us into your royal estate. Help us to walk in all You have planned for us in this hour.

Chapter 7

"In Holy Array"

Ascribe to the Lord, O sons of the mighty, ascribe to the Lord glory and strength. Give to the Lord the glory due to His name; worship the Lord in the beauty of holiness or in holy array.

Psalm 29:1-2

Ascribe to the Lord, you families of the peoples, ascribe to the Lord glory and strength, ascribe to the Lord the glory due His name. Bring an offering and come before Him; worship the Lord in the beauty of holiness and in holy array.

1 Chronicles 16:28-29

We, as God's people, the chosen of the Lord, are to give unto Him the glory that is due His name. All of the glory, the honor, the power and the majesty belong unto our Lord, and we are called to worship Him *"in the beauty of holiness."*

"Beauty," Strong's (#1927), means "decoration." We could then say, "Worship the Lord in decoration." That *Strong's* number refers to *Strong's* (#1926): "magnificence, i.e., ornament or splendor." This word *beauty,* then takes on the meaning of becom-

Worship is not an Outer Court experience!

ing "decorated magnificently," and it happens when we stand in the place of holiness and we worship the Lord Jesus Christ. It is as though we had become ornamentally clothed in His splendor.

Not an Outer Court Experience

Likening our experience to the physical layout of the Temple, worship is not an Outer Court experience. We experience praise in the Outer Court, but when we have made our spiritual procession into the Holy of Holies, then we are worshiping the Lord, the One who deserves all the worship we can render to Him.

In Old Testament times, something could be said of the priests as they made their procession from the Outer Court into the Inner Court, to the Holy Place and finally into the Holy of Holies. They were dressed magnificently, decorated in splendor. They were ornately decked, for their procession was before the King of Glory.

It was the Lord Himself who designed the garments of the priests. Down to the smallest detail, He dressed His priests exactly the way He wanted them to be when they entered His presence. The garments of those who ministered to the Lord in the beauty of holiness were *"for glory and for beauty"* (Exodus 28:2, KJV).

Dressed Magnificently

The Amplified Bible takes this thought a little further, when it suggests that we worship the Lord *"in the beauty of holiness and in holy array"* (1 Chronicles 16:29). This word *"array,"* according to *Webster's*, means "military order, battle array, a fighting force in battle order, ceremonial dress or outward adornment or to dress oneself magnificently." As we worship our Lord and Savior, we are dressed magnificently and are spiritually adorned, but we also become ceremonially dressed, fall militarily in order and are arrayed for battle.

Many times in recent months, as we have been worshiping the Lord and giving Him all the glory due to His name, we have become magnificently dressed by Him. Our shoes and our clothing have been sprinkled with gold dust or crystal or the dusting of some other beautiful stone, as the glory from Heaven covers us. When this has happened, many have also received the miracle of gold or platinum fillings in their teeth.

Why is this happening? As the worship of the saints ascends into the heavens, some of Heaven is being released back upon us, and God is dressing us to meet with Him. Even during the teaching of the Word of God, this heavenly dusting of God's glory falls to dress and adorn magnificently those who are in attendance.

Isaiah tells us to put on *"the garment of praise"* in place of *"the spirit of heaviness"* (Isaiah 61:3, KJV), and now is the time. We know that the Lord has given us spiritual garments in which we should be dressed, and *"the garment of praise"* is one of those necessary articles of clothing. When we put on His garments, we no longer look like the world or act like the world.

This word *garment* means "array or raiment." As we worship the Lord in the beauty of holiness and holy array, we will have beautiful garments of praise that clothe us. We are no longer clothed in heavy burdens and failing spirits. We are dressed magnificently, outwardly adorned by the dustings of Heaven—arrayed for battle.

Arrayed for Battle

As we worship the Lord in Spirit and in truth and with one heart, we become arrayed for battle, or we are set in military order. As we praise and worship our Creator, the Owner and Possessor of our souls (not as something that we do simply for fun or to make us feel good), things begin to transpire both in the heavens and in the earth. The earth is shaken, and the heavens are opened.

We are set in position as a great host, an army, whose principle officer is Jehovah Sabaoth. Jesus is the Captain of the Host, not only of the angels, who are the heavenly host, or the army of Heaven, and who cry "Holy! Holy! Holy!" around His throne day and night, worshiping Him, but He is also Jehovah Sabaoth, the Lord of the Battle, the Captain of the Army of God now positioned in the earth.

Some of our greatest battles will be won as we worship the Lord. Our greatest deliverances will come during our praise and worship to the Lord. Worship is one of our greatest weapons to use against the enemy:

> Let the saints be joyful in the glory and beauty [which God confers upon them]; let them sing for joy upon their beds. Let the high praises of God be in their throats and a two-edged sword in their hands, to wreak vengeance upon the nations and chastisement upon the peoples, to bind their kings with chains, and their nobles with fetters of iron, to execute upon them the judgment written. He [the Lord] is the honor of all His saints. Praise the Lord! (Hallelujah!)
>
> Psalm 149:5-9

The Lord confers upon us, His saints, *"glory and beauty."* Is this glory and beauty visible? Why not?

We are to be joyful in the glory. We are to let the high praises of God be in our mouths, even as we are to have the two-edged sword of God's Word in our hands. Praise is powerful.

When we sing the high praises of God, we will *"wreak vengeance upon"* the enemies of the land. Our praises will *"bind"* evil ruling powers with *"chains."* Instead of us being bound in spiritual fetters, we will bind spiritual ruling powers and place them in chains and fetters.

As you praise God, you are *"execut[ing] ... the judgment"* that has already been written against your spiritual enemies and the enemies of God. The Lord is our honor.

The King James Version renders this final phrase as: *"this honor have all his saints."* It is an honor to be given the ability to sing the high praises of Christ Jesus and have your praises destroy the powers of darkness. This sounds like the maneuvers of a great and powerful army, arrayed for battle, worshiping the Lord in the beauty of holiness or in holy array.

The Legitimate Bride

Kings' daughters are among Your honorable women; at Your right hand stands the queen in gold of Ophir.   Psalm 45:9

"*Queen,*" *Strong's* (7694 and 7695), means "the legitimate queen or the legitimate wife." The King's daughters are honorable women, and at His right hand stands the queen, the legitimate Bride. She is not a concubine, nor is she lawless, but she enjoys the full benefits of being the legitimate spouse.

It is only the legitimate wife who receives the full benefits of the marriage contract. In the same way, we, the Bride of Christ, will be able to experience the full benefits of our covenant with our soon-to-be Husband.

A concubine may be in love, but she has not entered into a marriage contract. She operates unlawfully. She is not committed, she may not be faithful, and she cannot be trusted. The legitimate bride, on the other hand, is faithful, committed, lawful and submitted, and she is under a binding contract—a marriage covenant that cannot be broken.

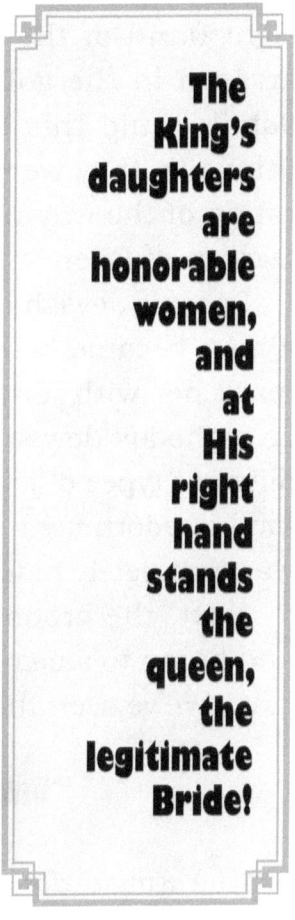

The King's daughters are honorable women, and at His right hand stands the queen, the legitimate Bride!

At your right hand stands the queen in the gold of Ophir. Psalm 45:9

The gold mining area known as Ophir was the richest gold region in the earth in ancient times, and was located in the Garden of Eden. The legitimate queen, the Bride of Christ, stands at the right hand of the King of Glory, and she stands arrayed in the gold of Ophir. Without going into detail, could this be part of the restoration of all things as they were back to God's people, a restoration of the way things were intended back in the Garden of Eden?

In some Jewish circles, the custom was that when a man became betrothed to a woman, he began to mark her with jewels. By the day of her marriage, an orthodox Jewish bride was literally covered with different types of jewels. She was so laden with every kind of adornment that much of her actual garment was completely hidden.

Next, the groom took liquid or pulverized gold and began to smear it on her face and other exposed skin. We've seen that manifestation too.

"Inwrought with Gold"

The King's daughter in the inner part [of the palace] is all glorious; her clothing is inwrought with gold. Psalm 45:13

Those who stand worshiping their King of Glory in the inner part of the palace (in our case, in the Holy of Holies), are *"all glorious." "Glorious,"* Strong's

(#3519 and #3520), means "glory, weightiness, magnificence, and wealth."

Her clothing is inwrought with gold.
Psalm 45:13

"Inwrought," Strong's (#4865), means "a (reticulated) setting of a gem." *Reticulated* means "to form a net or mesh appearance with gold; to encase gems in the mesh of gold." As the biblical bride stood in the palace (the Holy of Holies) worshiping her Lord and God, her clothing was inwrought with gold. It was reticulated as a gold net or mesh-like casing used for encasing gems.

In the same way, as we, the Lord's Bride-to-be, have stood in the inner chambers of the King's palace (the Holy of Holies), we have had our clothes inwrought with gold. It not only covers us; it also seems to be embedded into the fabric of our clothing. As we stand in the Holy of Holies worshiping the Lord of glory, our clothes begin to be covered in a beautiful dusting of His glory.

The threads of the fabric of our clothing looks just like the *Strong's* definition, and the dustings and the jewels are set into the threads of our clothing just as is described in Psalm 45:13. Her clothing was inwrought with gold as she stood in the Holy Place worshiping God, and we have experienced the very same thing as we have stood worshiping Him. The golden glory and the other beautiful colors God is sending have become inwrought, or worked into, our garments. What a blessing!

The Bride Is Preparing Herself

Let us rejoice and shout for joy [exulting and triumphant]! Let us celebrate and ascribe to Him glory and honor, for the marriage of the Lamb [at last] has come, and His bride has prepared herself.   Revelation 19:7

We are in a time of great preparation, as the Bride goes through the process of preparing herself for the marriage of the Lamb. This is not an overnight process, but a rather lengthy one. When the right time comes, there will be a great celebration, with rejoicing and shouting for joy, and there will be a great feast. At last, the Bride will be ready for the Marriage Supper of the Lamb! In preparation for this day, the Lord is allowing us to experience *The Glory of God Revealed.*

Father,

As we worship You in the beauty of holiness, You are dressing us magnificently. As we worship You, we are placed in military order. Jesus, it is our desire to be Your Bride, equipped and prepared for the day of Your return.

The Glory Releases Destiny

Chapter 8

A Call in the Wilderness

Now Moses kept the flock of Jethro, his father-in-law, the priest of Midian; and he led the flock to the back or west side of the wilderness, and came to Horeb or Sinai, the mountain of God. The Angel of the Lord appeared to him in a flame of fire out of the midst of a bush; and he looked, and behold the bush burned with fire, yet was not consumed. And Moses said, I will now turn aside and see this great sight, why the bush is not burned.   Exodus 3:1-3

Moses had been on the back side of the desert for forty years, and all hope of being the deliverer he knew he was called to be must now have been gone. Any confidence of great power, anointing or the slightest ability to speak had probably dwindled. But Moses was about to have an encounter with God, a visitation that would bring God's glory into his life and reveal his destiny.

Like Moses, many of us have been on the back side of the desert tending sheep. We had dreams, visions and thoughts of something greater. Our destinies were envisioned. As time has passed, however, the fulfillment of that destiny has never materialized. Now, we too need a visitation. Knowing that there must be more for us, many of us have cried out to God: "Show us Your glory! Revive Your Church, O Lord!" And just as Moses had an encounter with the living God, the Church is about to have a similar experience.

The glory of God would come to Moses in the form of a burning bush, and his life would be radically changed. It took a burning bush to get his attention. His dreams had died, his visions were no longer in sight, and no hope or thought of destiny fulfilled lay before him. His future seemed only to hold the hope of continuing to tend Jethro's flocks on the back side of the desert.

But the Dream Maker, the Vision Giver, the Destiny Fulfiller, was about to have an encounter with Moses, and the things that had died in the wilderness were about to come to life again. The days of awe and wonder that Moses was destined to be a part of from the foundations of the earth were about to overtake him. Broken, he could now be used and his destiny could be loosed.

A Burning Bush

There is a burning bush in our midst, and it is getting our attention. It is a divine visitation, and it is bringing a glory that will also loose our destinies. In fact, the greatest hour of destiny is upon the Church at this very moment.

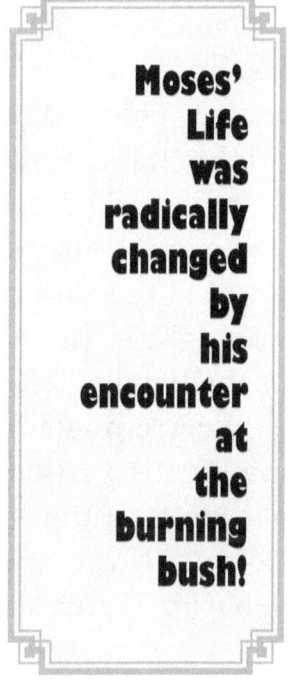

Moses' Life was radically changed by his encounter at the burning bush!

The Angel of the Lord appeared to him in a flame of fire out of the midst of a bush.
Exodus 3:2

This was not any ordinary angel. This was the pre-incarnate presence of Jesus. This was the Angel of God's Presence, the Angel of the Covenant, the Angel of Jehovah, who stood right in the middle of the flame.

Now we are experiencing our own burning bush. We have been on the back side of the desert, waiting for something to take place. We have cried out to the Lord, "Fulfill our destinies," "show us Your glory" and "bring a visitation of Your presence to us." Suddenly we find ourselves under divine visitation, with the glory of God in our midst, and we realize that our destinies are about to be loosed.

Our burning bush is the visible, manifested presence of God's glory, the glory that is being displayed in the earth. The Angel of the Lord, the Angel of the Covenant, the Angel of His Presence, is right in the middle of the glory, in the middle of the flame.

This word "*flame*," *Strong's* (#3827 and #3851), means "a flaming head of a spear, to gleam, a flash, a sharply polished blade or point of a weapon, a blade, bright, flame, glittering." This flame was like the flaming head of a spear. It gleamed, it flashed like a sharply polished blade, and it glittered. And the Angel of the Covenant, the Angel of God's Presence, was right in the middle of this flame that gleamed, flashed and glittered.

We are now under divine visitation, and God is manifesting His presence. It gleams, it flashes, it glitters, and the Angel of the Lord, the Angel of the Covenant, the Angel of His Presence, the Angel of Jehovah, is right in the middle of it.

Turning Aside

Just as the Lord used Moses' day of visitation to get his attention, I believe the Lord is trying to get the attention of His people today. We must be willing to respond. Moses was required to do something, just as we will be required to respond. The call must be answered. There simply must be a response on our part.

Moses could have said, "Isn't that interesting?" and kept on walking, and he would have missed the day of his visitation. If he had, he would have missed the days of awe and wonder and missed the fulfillment of his destiny too.

The Lord may call, but it is always up to us to answer that call. There always needs to be a response from us.

The visitation is here, the glory is here, and the call is going out. Now, we must respond.

And Moses said, I will now turn aside and see this great sight. Exodus 3:3

Moses did not just keep on walking. He turned aside to see this great sight. This word *"sight,"* *Strong's* (#4758), means "an appearance (the thing seen), to see if it is real, comeliness, the looks, the vision, the appearance, beautiful, countenance, fair, favored, form, to look upon." In *Strong's* (#7200), it means "to perceive, consider, discern, make to enjoy, have experience, gaze joyfully, look on one another, mark, regard, have respect, see one another, show self, spy, stare, view." When Moses turned to see this great sight, it meant that he had to look at the appearance of the thing seen. He had to see if it was real. What he saw was the beauty of it, its fair, favored form. He had to look upon it. He had to consider it, discern it, enjoy it, have and experience it and gaze joyfully at it.

As we are turning aside to the manifested presence of the Lord in our midst and seeing this great sight, we are looking at the appearance of it and the beauty of it. We are looking to see if it is real. More than that, we perceive that it is God, just as Moses had to decide that in the midst of the glittering flame was the Angel of the Lord. We are discerning it, enjoying it, having an experience, gazing at it joyfully, looking at one another, having respect for it, showing self, staring at it and viewing it.

How awesome that it comes from the Lord and He gives us the liberty to enjoy it! How awesome that the simple meaning of the word *sight* could set us free to turn aside to this beautiful visible glory. We have a burning bush in the midst of our wilderness, and the Lord is saying that it is okay for us to take pleasure in it. We are experiencing *The Glory of God Revealed.*

Lord,

We will now turn aside to see this wondrous sight. You, O Lord, are in the midst of it, and our destinies await us in You.

Chapter 9

A Call in Captivity

*Now [when I was] in [my] thirtieth year, in the
fourth month, in the fifth day of the month, as
I was in the midst of captivity beside the river
Chebar [in Babylonia], the heavens were opened
and I saw visions of God.* Ezekiel 1:1

Many of the great patriarchs, prophets and polit-
ical leaders of Bible days had a similar experience.
They were living fairly routine daily lives ... until they
suddenly began seeing visions of Heaven, visions of
God and visions of His glory. At that point, they were
catapulted into a whole new realm of ministry and
responsibility. And the same is happening with us.

In the case of Ezekiel, he was born into a priest-
ly family and grew up around the daily activities of

the temple in Jerusalem, so he had a godly heritage. But then he was exiled from his native land and taken into captivity in Babylonia, along with many others of his people. There in that forbidding place, the young prophet was at the River Chebar one day when suddenly the heavens opened to him. Just as Moses had been on the backside of the desert when His divine visitation came, Ezekiel was in captivity when he first saw the glory of God and experienced the loosing of his destiny.

To make things worse, Ezekiel was among these evil Chaldeans!

Called by God

The word of the Lord came expressly to Ezekiel the priest, the son of Buzi, in the land of the Chaldeans by the river Chebar.   Ezekiel 1:3

Ezekiel was not only far from his beloved Jerusalem, having been taken captive by the Babylonians, but he was also now living in the land of the Chaldeans. This word *"Chaldeans"* simply means "demons, devils and destroyers." It was bad enough to be in captivity and to be exiled from the Holy City, but to make things worse, he was among these evil Chaldeans.

You may know what Ezekiel was feeling about that time, for you may have been on the back side of the desert recently. Maybe you, too, have felt like you were in captivity and even that there were a few demons, devils or destroyers around.

Some of us have only a valley view. We can only see what is within our confined space. But don't despair. Those who have been in the valley are prime candidates for an encounter with God. A valley is a place of breakthrough, a place of hatching. If that is where you find yourself today, you are in the right place for the Lord to move mightily in your life.

God's Plan Cannot Be Stopped

When God begins to move, there is no oppression, no captivity, no demon, no Babylonian and no Chaldean that can hinder what He is doing. When God's glory is revealed, our destinies will also be revealed.

In the midst of the great oppression of Babylon, Ezekiel sensed a window open in Heaven, He began to see visions of the glory, and the voice of the Lord came to him. This is happening again today, and nothing can stop what the Lord is doing in the earth.

Many times we find ourselves in situations that constrain our ability to believe that the Lord will move on our behalf. A wilderness experience is just one of those times. Our wilderness seasons are sometimes so prolonged that we cannot imagine the Lord ever doing anything else with us again.

Being in captivity, with the Chaldeans encamped all around us, just as Ezekiel experienced, is another of those times. Whatever your situation is today, know that God is right there with you. Over and over, throughout the Word of God, we see Him moving in the midst of some of the most hopeless situations. Divine visitation often comes in our bleakest hour. When all hope is gone of any deliverance or of any change occurring, the God of glory can suddenly come.

It does not matter if you have been on the backside of the desert for forty years, or if you feel you have been led into captivity and are surrounded by the Chaldeans. A day of visitation has come upon the earth. God's presence and His glory are in our midst, and destinies are about to be loosed. The Chaldeans cannot stop what the Lord is about to do in the earth—with His people and through His people.

An Open Heaven

The heavens were opened and I saw visions of God.   Ezekiel 1:1

The prophet Ezekiel, even though he was in captivity and was among demons, devils and destroyers, had an open window to Heaven and saw heavenly visions of God's presence and His glory. These visions of God were His manifested presence. They were visions of His glory.

First the divine presence came, then visions of the glory came, and finally destiny was loosed upon Ezekiel as he yielded to it. This young man was suddenly loosed into the very purpose for which he had been born into this world—to become a prophet and a visionary, to uproot the evil of his day and to foresee and declare a day yet to come.

Ezekiel had visions of a temple never before seen, of a river of anointing issuing out of a temple whose threshold had been filled with the Shekinah, of a valley of dried, scattered bones that came to life and became a great and powerful army in the earth, and he had visions of the glory that we are even now experiencing. I suggest to you that he was foreseeing the very days in which we are now living.

As he waited upon God, there in the midst of great idolatry, destruction, bondage and even God's judgment, he received not only an open window of Heaven, but also God's divine presence through revelations of His glory. It is no wonder that, just like Moses, Ezekiel's true destiny was loosed when the glory came.

You cannot separate God's presence from the glory. They are one and the same. When the presence of the Lord comes, the glory is there, and when the glory is manifested, the presence of the Lord is there. In fact, the beauty of the glory is not only in its magnificent and glorious appearance, but in the fact that God is in it.

The presence of the Lord and His glory come because He has a plan and wants to loose us into our destinies. We are His co-laborers, and if we are to labor with Him, then we must be thrust into the vineyard and loosed into our destinies.

In this way, Ezekiel was thrust into his vineyard, just as Moses, Gideon, Isaiah, Jeremiah and many others had been before him. First came visions of God, visions of Heaven and visions of divine glory, and then came the thrusting forth. And it is no different for us.

Now Ezekiel's open window was before him, as is ours today, in this grand and glorious birthing of a new day of awe and wonder upon the earth. There is a divine purpose in us seeing *The Glory of God Revealed*.

Father,

We are at the River Chebar, the place of seeing the glory. There are no Chaldeans, devils, demons nor destroyers that can stop what You are doing in the earth. Nothing and no one can stop Your glory and Your divine destiny from being loosed upon Your people in this hour!

Chapter 10

Visions of Divine Glory

The heavens were opened and I saw visions of God.

As I looked, behold, a stormy wind came out of the north, and a great cloud with a fire enveloping it and flashing continually; a brightness was about it and out of the midst of it there seemed to glow amber metal, out of the midst of the fire.

As to the appearance of the wheels and their construction: in appearance they gleamed like chrysolite; and the four were formed alike, and their construction work was as it were a wheel within a wheel.

Over the head of the [combined] living creature there was the likeness of a firmament, looking like the terrible and awesome [dazzling of shin-

ing] crystal or ice stretched across the expanse of the sky over their heads.

And above the firmament that was over their heads was the likeness of a throne in appearance like a sapphire stone, and seated above the likeness of a throne was a likeness with the appearance of a Man. From what had the appearance of His waist upward, I saw a lustre as it were glowing metal with the appearance of fire enclosed round about within it; and from the appearance of His waist downward, I saw as it were the appearance of fire, and there was brightness [of a halo] round about Him. Like the appearance of the bow that is in the cloud on the day of rain, so was the appearance of the brightness round about. This was the appearance of the likeness of the glory of the Lord. And when I saw it, I fell upon my face and I heard a voice of One speaking.

Ezekiel 1:1, 4, 16, 22 and 26-28

As we saw in the last chapter, Ezekiel was at the River Chebar—the place of seeing the glory. He had been brought into captivity, along with many others from his nation. His circumstances were not what we would consider to be conducive to a move of God in his life, and yet in the midst of his captivity, there came a visitation from the Lord. The heavens were opened, and Ezekiel saw visions of Heaven's glory.

The Heavens Were Opened

"Heavens," Strong's (#8064), simply means the "air" or the "sky." *"Opened," Strong's* (#6605), means "to open wide, loosen, let go free, unstop, ungird." *"Vision," Strong's* (#4759 and #4758), means "a mirror, a looking glass, a view, the act of seeing, an appearance." The heavens were opened wide, loosed, unstopped and ungirded, and there was a vision. Ezekiel had the ability to see, as if he was looking into a mirror or a looking glass, and there was an appearance of God.

The glory of God's presence was upon Ezekiel, and the closer His presence came to Ezekiel, the greater the glory he experienced. Or should we say, perhaps, that the closer Ezekiel got to the Lord, the greater the glory he experienced. It works both ways, and it is the same for you and me. The closer we get to God's presence, the greater the glory we will see!

As we press in to His heavenly dwelling place, the Holy of Holies, He presses in to us. We must choose

> Ezekiel's circumstances were not what we would consider to be conducive to a move of God in his life!

to press in to Him, to press in to His holy presence, to press in to His Holy of Holies, and not settle for anything less. Whether it is in our praise, our worship or the anointing while preaching His Word, we must choose the very best. As Sister Ruth Heflin always said, "We praise till the worship comes, we worship till the glory comes, and then we stand in the glory."

God in the Whirlwind

As I looked, behold, a stormy wind came out of the north.   Ezekiel 1:4

This *"stormy wind"* is translated *"whirlwind"* in the King James Version of the Bible. In *Strong's* (7307), we see the Hebrew word used here, *rûwach*, means "wind; by resemblance breath, sensible (or even violent) exhalation, life, air, anger, unsubstantiality; a region of the sky; by resemblance spirit, courage, mind, blast, whirlwind." In *Strong's* (5591) it means "hurricane, stormy, tempest," from (5590), "to toss with a tempest, be sore troubled, scatter with a whirlwind."

This stormy wind, this whirlwind that came, was the very *rûwach,* or the breath, of God, and it came from the north, or from a gloomy unknown quarter. The glory many times is likened to a whirlwind in the Scriptures. This powerful force that took on the form of a stormy wind is the very breath of God.

The Wind of Judgment

A whirlwind can also be a sign of judgment:

Behold, the tempest of the Lord has gone forth with wrath, a sweeping and gathering tempest; it shall whirl and burst upon the heads of the wicked.   Jeremiah 30:23

When the wind, or the whirlwind, of God, which is a tempest, or a storm, comes to the wicked, the unrighteous, the mockers of God, there is judgment. When these winds blow, things happen, and destruction inevitably comes.

Winds of Change and Blessing

There are also winds of God that come to blow upon those who are His, those who are in right standing. In this case, they are winds of blessing to His people, and they bring change into our lives. This is always for our good.

Zechariah spoke of windstorms that come as the Lord is restoring double to His people. In these windstorms, the Lord becomes the Lord of our battles. He becomes our defense and protection. At the same time, to our enemies, He is a destructive force, rendering judgment:

As for you also, because of and for the sake of the [covenant of the Lord with His people, which was sealed with sprinkled] covenant blood, I have released and sent forth your imprisoned people out of the waterless pit. Return to the stronghold [of security and prosperity],

God will restore what the enemy has tried to steal, and He will fulfill your destiny!

you prisoners of hope; even today do I declare that I will restore double your former prosperity to you.

And the Lord shall be seen over them and His arrow shall go forth as the lightning, and the Lord God will blow the trumpet and will go forth in the windstorms of the south. The Lord of hosts shall defend and protect them; and they shall devour and they shall tread on [their fallen enemies] ... and they shall drink [of victory] and be noisy and turbulent as from wine and become full like bowls ... like the corners of the [sacrificial] altar. And the Lord their God will save them on that day as the flock of His people, for they shall be as the [precious] jewels of a crown, lifted high over and shining glitteringly upon His land.

Zechariah 9:11-12 and 14-16

I can't help but feel that this is a word for today. Because of the covenant the Lord has with us, a covenant sealed in the blood of Jesus, He will release all those who are in the waterless pit. In other words, it is bad enough to be in a pit, but when it is waterless, it is even worse.

When Joseph was stripped of his garment (representing his anointing) and was thrown into a pit, it was a waterless pit. The enemy of his soul wanted to stop his destiny. Many times the enemy will come to strip you of your anointing and try to stop your destiny. It will be as though you have been thrown into a waterless pit. But the Lord says, "Because you are Mine, and I am in covenant with you, I will deliver you from the waterless pit" (see Zechariah (9:11). Our God will restore what the enemy has tried to steal from you, and He will also fulfill your destiny!

The Lord went on to declare a return to security and prosperity for those who have clung to hope so long that they have become prisoners of hope. If that is you, you need no longer just cling to hope. You will now have a stronghold of security and prosperity, and the Lord will restore to you twice as much as you have lost.

I believe that this is the season of the double blessing—"double for your trouble." Double the inheritance! Double the increase! Double the anointing!

The Lord has promised to be over His people, and He will blow the trumpet. The trumpet of the Old

Testament was the *shofar.* This is the Jubilee horn that He will blow to release blessings upon us and destroy our enemies.

Then He will go forth in the windstorms, and He will defend and protect His own. His people will destroy their enemies and drink the cup of victory. And, in that day, salvation will come. God's people will be the precious jewels of a crown, shining glitteringly upon His land.

This word *"crown," Strong's* (#5145 and #5144), means "set apart, dedication (of a priest or Nazarite), crown of royalty, consecration, separation, to abstain (from food and drink, from impurity), to be set apart for sacred purposes." This is a crown of righteousness, a crown of right standing with the Lord.

A Cloud of God's Glory and His Presence

And a great cloud with a fire enveloping it and flashing continually; a brightness was about it.
Ezekiel 1:4

From the time that Israel was delivered out of the hand of Pharaoh and during the march through the wilderness, God revealed Himself to the people in a cloud by day and in a fire by night:

The Lord went before them by day in a pillar of cloud to lead them along the way and by night in a pillar of fire to give them light, that they might travel by day and by night.   Exodus 13:21

To the people of Israel, the cloud of God's presence was a protection and a light in their darkness, but to their enemies it was a darkness and a frightening terror.

> *And the Angel of God Who went before the host of Israel moved and went behind them; and the pillar of the cloud went from before them and stood behind them, coming between the host of Egypt and the host of Israel. It was a cloud and darkness to the Egyptians, but it gave light by night to the Israelites; and the one host came not near the other all night.*   Exodus 14:19-20

When the children of Israel saw the cloud of God's presence (with the Angel of His presence) that was leading them suddenly move to the rear of the camp, I am sure they must have been concerned about what was taking place. They soon discovered that the Lord had their best interests in mind. To God's people, His presence, manifested in the cloud of His presence, was a protection and a safeguard, but to the enemies of God and the enemies of God's people, it was judgment and terror.

It was the same with the windstorm. To those who are in Christ Jesus, it is blessing, but to those who are not in Him, it is judgment.

> *Behold, the glory of the Lord appeared in the cloud!*   Exodus 16:10

This makes it very clear that the glory was in the cloud.

> *Then the cloud [the Shekinah, God's visible presence] covered the Tent of Meeting, and the glory of the Lord filled the tabernacle!*
>
> Exodus 40:34

Here we see the cloud as the visible presence of the Lord. It covered the Tent of Meeting, and the glory filled the Tabernacle.

Ezekiel had a vision of the glory of God, the whirlwind came, and a great cloud with fire enveloped it. To Ezekiel, it was the presence of the Lord, His glory. To those around Him who were under judgment, it would have been darkness and gloom.

A Polished Spectrum of Color

> *Out of the midst of it there seemed to glow amber metal, out of the midst of the fire.* Ezekiel 1:4

There was the appearance of a glowing metal the color of amber. *"Amber," Strong's* (#2830), means "bronze or polished spectrum metal." Metals have luster, and a spectrum is a band of colors. *Luster* is "radiance, brightness and splendor." The luster that comes from a metal or a mineral is determined by the quality or type of light that is shined on it and by the intensity of that light. I believe that Ezekiel saw a beautiful band of colors, a multifaceted spectrum of color, having luster, radiance and brightness. As light was shining on it, or reflecting off of it, it gave forth a wonderful display of color that was jewel-like.

The beautiful dustings of glory that now come in a full spectrum of lustrous colors are the glory of God, His presence, manifested upon His people.

A Wheel within a Wheel

As to the appearance of the wheels and their construction: in appearance they gleamed like chrysolite; and the four were formed alike, and their construction work was as it were a wheel within a wheel. Ezekiel 1:16

The King James Version of the Bible translates this word *"chrysolite"* as *"beryl."* This word *"beryl," Strong's* (8658), means "a topaz." A chrysolite is a beryl, which is also a topaz.

We know that the four living creatures, mentioned before verse 16, are four portraits of Jesus that relate to the four gospels.

The beautiful dustings of glory that come in a full spectrum of lustrous colors are the glory of God!

Matthew represents our Lord as the King [the lion], Mark portrays Him as the Servant [the ox], Luke represents Him in His humanity [the man], and John declares His deity [the eagle]. There is a wheel within a wheel, which also represents the Father and the Son. It is the *rûwach,* the Holy Spirit, which moves the wheel.

> *And they went every one straight forward; wherever the spirit would go, they went.*
> *Wherever the spirit went, the creatures went and the wheels rose along with them, for the spirit or life of the [four living creatures acting as one] living creature was in the wheels.* Ezekiel 1:12 and 20

The four faces of the living creatures represent Jesus. The wheel within the wheel represents the Father and the Son, and the Holy Spirit is in the wheels. The spirit of life was in the wheels, and wherever the spirit [the *rûwach*] would move, the whole wheel would move.

Ezekiel was about to be loosed into His ultimate destiny. The divine presence of the Most High God was before him, as the glory of the Lord Jesus Christ was also before him.

A Sheet of Crystal (and Gold?)

Over the head of the [combined] living creature there was the likeness of a firmament, looking like the terrible and awesome [dazzling of shining] crystal or ice stretched across the expanse of sky over their heads.   Ezekiel 1:22

This is very exciting! This word *"firmament,"* *Strong's* (#7549 and #7554), is the word *raqiyah.* The *firmament,* or the *raqiyah,* means "to compress or pound together, to pound the earth as a sign of passion, to expand by hammering, an arch of the sky, firmament, to overlay with thin sheets of metal." Believing scientists have declared that the firmament described by the book of Genesis was a canopy of compressed metals, thin sheets of crystal, and a thin sheet of transparent gold. What Ezekiel saw in his visions of divine glory lines up with that exactly: The firmament looked to him *"like the terrible and awesome [dazzling of shining] crystal or ice stretched across the sky"* over the heads of the creatures.

This word *"crystal,"* *Strong's* (#7140), means "ice (as if bald, i.e., smooth), rock crystal." I described in a previous chapter the smooth, bald, crystalline topaz stones that have been manifested in our meetings.

I believe that what Ezekiel was seeing were some of the same things we are now being blessed to see. In one way, it's nothing new. The Bible tells us that our God *"is [always] the same, yesterday, [yes] and forever [to the ages]"* (Hebrews 13:8), and Ecclesiastes declares: *"There is nothing new under the sun"* (Ecclesiastes 1:9). It is only new to us.

Ezekiel's vision continued:

From what had the appearance of His waist upward, I saw a lustre as it were glowing metal

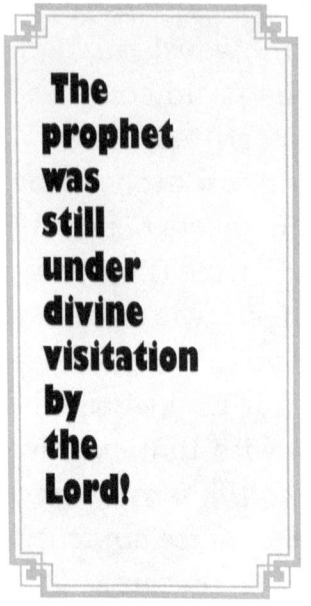

The prophet was still under divine visitation by the Lord!

with the appearance of fire enclosed round about within it; and from the appearance of His waist downward, I saw as it were the appearance of fire, and there was brightness [of a halo] round about Him. Like the appearance of the bow that is in the cloud on the day of rain, so was the appearance of the brightness round about. This was the appearance of the likeness of the glory of the Lord. And when I saw it, I fell upon my face and I heard a voice of One speaking. Ezekiel 1:27-28

The prophet was still under divine visitation by the Lord. He had seen the Lord and His glory. He had seen God's divine presence and the manifestation of His glory, not only coming to the earth, but also coming to him personally. The next thing that transpired was Ezekiel's commissioning by the Lord.

In order for the prophet to be brought into his destiny, he would have vision of Heaven, visions of God and visions of His glory. And what did it all mean? It meant that God was revealing Himself, manifesting His presence and His glory with the intent of developing His purposes in the earth. What we have seen here was just the beginning of many revelations and many experiences that would thrust the man of God into his great destiny. And it all came about as a result of *The Glory of God Revealed.*

Lord,

As You are opening the windows of Heaven, and we are experiencing Your glory, open our eyes to see all that You have for us. Father, as Your Spirit is moving in the earth, let us always remain in right standing with You. Let Your rûwach blow over us afresh and anew, and let the cloud of Your presence rest upon us!

Chapter 11

Those Who Wait

Why, O Jacob, do you say, and declare, O Israel, My way and my lot are hidden from the Lord, and my right is passed over without regard from my God? Have you not known? Have you not heard? The everlasting God, the Lord, the Creator of the ends of the earth, does not faint or grow weary; there is no searching of His understanding. He gives power to the faint and weary, and to him who has no might He increases strength [causing it to multiply and making it to abound]. Even youths shall faint and be weary, and [selected] young men shall feebly stumble and fall exhausted; but THOSE WHO WAIT for the Lord [who expect, look for, and hope in Him] shall change and renew their strength and power. Isaiah 40:27-31

Have you ever felt that the Lord did not understand what is going on in your life or that you were somehow hidden from His sight? There are times when it seems as though we have been stripped of all of our rights and that the Lord is not even giving a second glance at all of our distresses.

> **When a strong rope is bound together with a weak string, the rope lends the string its strength!**

The Lord Is Never Weary

We may grow weary and tired, but the Lord does not. If we are faint or weary and have no more strength, He will give us His power and strength, until it multiplies and abounds. Isaiah gave us the key. It is to be found in waiting for the Lord.

"Wait," Strong's (#6960), means "to bind together by twisting, collect; to expect, to gather together, look, patiently, tarry, wait (for, on, upon)." So many times, as Christians, we become weak, weary, exhausted, faint or discouraged, and we find ourselves sitting back, pulling back and waiting ... and waiting ... and waiting. All the time that we are waiting ... and waiting

... and waiting, the Lord is waiting for us to do something. The Lord has eternity to wait for us, but when we find ourselves waiting ... and waiting ... and waiting, we have lost precious time in the Kingdom.

I believe the Lord meant something quite different with this word *wait*. There *are* times that we must wait. There *are* seasons for everything, and when it is not the Lord's timing or season to move, we must wait. But I also believe that when we are weary, or faint, weak, exhausted or discouraged, all we have to do is bind together with the Lord and get twisted together with Him. There is strength to be found in Him.

Bound and Twisted together with God

When a strong rope is bound and twisted together with a weak string, the rope lends the string its strength. The piece of string, by itself, has no strength, and it is vulnerable to breaking. It is weak and cannot resist much of anything that might pull on it. But if you take that weak piece of string, and you bind it together with the rope, then the weak, frail, vulnerable-to-breaking string begins to take on a strength it could never have had on its own.

Once the string is bound and twisted together with the rope, it is no longer weak or frail. The piece of string has now taken on the characteristics of the rope. It can be pulled on, yanked on and used. Great pressure can be put on it, and it will not break. It is now functioning with the strength of that with which it is twisted together. When we become bound and twisted together with the Lord, we are given strength, just as the weak string is strengthened by the rope.

Weakness, frailty or vulnerability to breaking is no longer operating in that piece of string. It has now changed its ability. It is now strong because it is twisted together, collected together, braided together with something strong. It is plaited together and interwoven with qualities it did not previously have.

It did not take long for the characteristics of that string to change. The moment it was twisted together with the strength of the rope, great change began to take place.

No Matter How Weak We Feel

It is the same for us. No matter how weak, weary or frail we have become from being pulled on, yanked on or stretched, the minute we decide to get twisted together with the Lord, the minute we begin to bind ourselves together with Him, we are no longer weak, frail, weary, exhausted, faint or on the verge of breaking. We begin to take on His characteristics. We become strong because He is strong.

Through the centuries, many people have learned the secret of waiting on the Lord. As we have seen, Ezekiel learned it at the River Chebar while in captivity in Babylonia: *"I was in the midst of captivity beside the river Chebar [in Babylonia], [when] the heavens were opened and I saw visions of God"* (Ezekiel 1:1).

According to *Strong's* (#3527), *"Chebar"* means "to plait together, braided, interwoven, to augment, (especially in number or quantity, to accumulate) in abundance, multiply." The first meaning—plaited together, braided together, interwoven with—brings us to a couple of different scriptures in which Ezekiel, before entering into that great realm of the glory, learned to wait. Remember that Ezekiel was at Chebar, the place of plaiting together, being interwoven together, braided together, with God.

Ezekiel Achieved His Full Destiny

One of the meanings of *"Chebar"* is very similar to the meaning of *"wait"* in Isaiah 40:31. They almost mean the same thing. Ezekiel would not have entered into the fullness of what the Lord had for him had he not walked in the divine principles set before him at the River Chebar.

Since Chebar was the place of plaiting together, being interwoven together, braided together, there was a process in motion that Ezekiel would have to comprehend. Being in exile, in Babylonian captivity and among the Chaldeans could have been quite a harsh experience—to say the least. Things were very difficult for Ezekiel, and I am sure that confusion, weariness, discouragement, hopelessness and many other feelings entered into the hearts of all those who belonged to the true and living God, as they suffered in servitude to Babylon.

Ezekiel—in exile, in captivity and among the Chaldeans—must have felt this way. He was probably weary and exhausted from the great journey and perhaps even overwhelmed by all he saw, so that it caused him to be a little fainthearted, confused or distressed. This young prophet, though, went right ahead with the plans and purposes of the Lord. In all of it, Ezekiel did not seem to miss a beat.

Ezekiel could have missed the day of his visitation if he had focused on his disappointments, on the Chaldeans, on his captivity, or on his weariness. He may have even wondered if the Lord was in control or if the Lord had even noticed the condition of His people. Ezekiel felt everything expressed by Isaiah 40:27-31, and yet he had a truth somehow locked inside his heart that allowed him to comprehend all that the Lord was doing in his life in that hour.

What was happening was not just for Ezekiel. It was for his nation, and it was for us and our nations today. It was for all of those who are called into the Kingdom for a time such as this.

But those who wait for the Lord [who expect, look for, and hope in Him] shall change and RENEW their strength and power.

Isaiah 40:31, Emphasis Added

What It Means to Be Renewed

"Renew," according to *Strong's* (#2498), means "to slide by, to hasten away, pass on, spring up, pierce or change: abolish, alter, change, cut off, go on forward, grow up, be over, pass (away, on, through), renew, sprout, strike through." Those who wait upon the Lord, those who bind together, who are roped together with the Lord by twisting, those who are braided together, plaited together, those who get connected with Him, shall renew their strength.

In other words, when we quit waiting for God to do something, and we get connected with Him, our strength will be renewed. With the *Strong's* (#2498) definition of *renew* and the scripture in Isaiah 40:31, we gain a new perspective on the words: *"shall renew their strength."* Your weakness, discouragement, faintheartedness and confusion will slide by. It will hasten away. It will pass on. Your strength will be renewed. Your strength will spring up and pierce through. It will change. Your weakness will be altered. It will be abolished. Your weakness will be cut off. You will go forward. You will grow up. Your

When we get connected with God, our strength will be renewed!

weakness will be over. Your feelings of weariness in well doing and your faintness will pass away. You will be renewed with strength that will sprout up and strike through and give you victory.

When something springs up, pierces through, is altered or is abolished, that sounds to me as if something immediately begins to take place. Praise God! How could we not get excited about this powerful revelation?

Yes, there are times when we must wait, but there are times when God is waiting for us to get connected to Him. When we do this, we are instantly renewed. There are some healings that manifest instantly, and then there are those that take a more gradual process. There are seasons and times of waiting upon God for our ministries. There are definitely seasons of waiting upon the Lord for direction. There are things in the Kingdom that will take place only when the Lord says so or when He allows them to be loosed into our lives—no matter what we do. In this sense, we do have to wait.

But in this passage of scripture, the Lord is talking about weakness, weariness and faintness that can overtake those who are His. If Ezekiel had not been connected to the Lord as the words *wait* and *Chebar* indicate to us, the ministry that transpired through this prophet might never have taken place. It was not a time for weariness, weakness and faintheartedness. When the Lord speaks to us to go and do, He requires us to move without hesitation—

regardless of the circumstances.

Some of those with the greatest unfulfilled destinies are waiting on the Lord, and yet He is waiting on them.

> *They that WAIT upon the* LORD *shall RENEW their strength.*
> Isaiah 40:31, KJV, Emphasis Added

Allow the Lord to give you *The Glory of God Revealed.*

Father,

We are in a day of great visitation, and You are bringing us to the place of seeing Your glory. Help us to learn Your principle of being yoked together with You, that we might spring up and shoot forth into the fullness You have planned for our lives! Lord, Your people have been waiting on You, but help us to understand that You are waiting on us!

Part III

The Glory Brings Increase

Chapter 12

A Growing River

The word of the Lord came expressly to Ezekiel the priest, the son of Buzi, in the land of the Chaldeans by the river Chebar; and the hand of the Lord was there upon him.   Ezekiel 1:3

The River Chebar, as we have seen, is where the revelation of the glory and a connecting with God came for Ezekiel. Now we will see that it was also a place of enlargement and increase.

"Chebar," according to *Strong's* (#3527), means "to augment (especially in number or quantity, to accumulate) in abundance, multiply." *Augment,* according to *Webster's*, means "to increase, grow larger, as a stream augments into a river, capable of increase, enlarge in size, to swell, make bigger."

An army augments, or grows larger, by adding rein-
forcements.

As we stand at the banks of the River Chebar, the
glory comes, we are yoked with the Lord and then the
augmentation begins. The streams of the glory and of
the river of God will begin to augment, increase, grow
larger. The streams of God's glory are about to change
into powerful rivers. And just as the streams increase
to rivers, the rivers are capable of increasing, enlarg-
ing in size, swelling, becoming bigger.

We are just in the beginning stages of what the
Lord is doing in this revival of the glory. There are
streams of God's glory flowing, but there is an augmentation that is also taking place. The streams of
anointing, of the glory, healing, signs and wonders
and miracles will now increase and enlarge until
they are no longer streams, but mighty, powerful
rivers flowing throughout the land.

> *Waters issued out from under the threshold of
> the temple toward the east ... , and, behold,
> waters were running out on the right side. ...
> And he caused me to pass through the waters,
> waters that were ankle-deep ... , and caused me
> to pass through the waters, waters that reached
> to the knees ... , and caused me to pass through
> the waters, waters that reached to the loins ...,
> for the waters had risen, waters to swim in, a
> river that could not be passed over or through.*
>
> Ezekiel 47:1-5

A Growing River

These were augmenting waters. They increased and became larger. They issued out from under the threshold of the Temple as a trickle, but then they grew until they were *"waters to swim in"* and *"a river that could not be passed over or through."*

By verse five, the water had risen. It was no longer ankle-deep, knee-deep nor loin-deep, but there were now waters to swim in. The waters of the river had augmented.

This word *"risen,"* according to *Strong's* (#1342), means "to mount up, to rise, (figuratively) be majestic, gloriously, grow up, increase, be risen, triumph."

These waters were augmented. They were not only increased in size and depth, but also risen to a new degree of power. They had risen and had become majestic, glorious and triumphant. They were majestic in that they were full of God's majesty. They were glorious in that they were full of His glory. They were triumphant in that they were full of His victory.

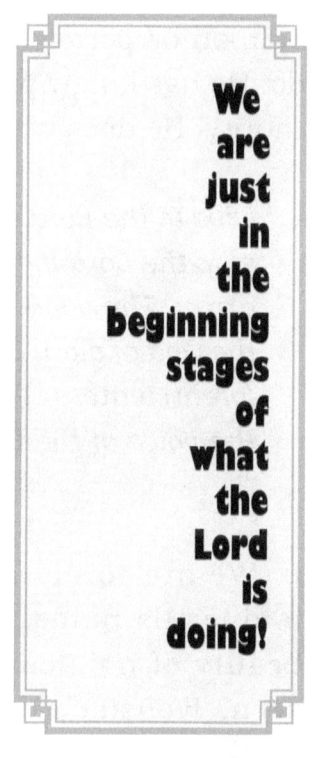

We are just in the beginning stages of what the Lord is doing!

Majestic Waters

Majestic waters speak of royal waters, or Kingdom waters, for they flow from the King of kings.

They are filled with sovereign power flowing from the sovereignty of God, from His kingly, or royal, powers. The sovereignty of God flows, or operates, on our behalf because He is the King over the Kingdom.

He is the sovereign ruler, and because of it He has kingly prerogatives. This means that He will move in sovereign power, with miracles and wonders, just because He wants to. He does not have to ask our opinion or permission about anything He wants to do. He has kingly prerogatives. He rules. He is in authority! He does what He will.

Give to the Lord the glory due to His name; worship the Lord in the beauty of holiness or in holy array. The voice of the Lord is upon the waters; the God of glory thunders; the Lord is upon many (great) waters. The voice of the Lord is powerful; the voice of the Lord is full of majesty.

Psalm 29:2-4

We are to give to the Lord all the glory that is due His name. We are to worship Him in the beauty of holiness, or in holy array. As we have seen, *Webster's* defines *array* as "military order, battle array; a fighting force in battle order, ceremonial dress or outward adornment, to dress oneself magnificently." We come into God's presence, giving Him all the glory, arrayed in military order, as a fighting force in battle order, ceremonially dressed, dressed magnificently. As we are coming into His presence, He is dressing us and adorning us magnificently.

Verse 3 then tells us that *"the voice of the Lord is upon the waters; the God of glory thunders; the Lord is upon many (great) waters."* Upon these waters, where the Lord is speaking and thundering, His voice is majestic (as we see in verse 4). And these are augmenting waters, as verse 3 shows: there are *"many (great) waters."*

I want you to see clearly what is happening upon these *"many (great) waters,"* these magnificent waters, these augmenting waters. The Lord of Glory dresses His Bride magnificently. His voice is in the waters, and He thunders. If the Lord's voice is upon the waters, He is speaking. When He thunders, He is rising against our enemies, speaking against them and declaring to them: "It is enough!"

Verse 7 says something that I find very interesting: *"The voice of the Lord splits and flashes forth forked lightning."* Upon these augmenting, risen, many (great) waters, the voice of the Lord *"splits and flashes forth forked lightning."* Lightning speaks of revelation. As I have said, in many of our glory revival meetings, we have seen golden sparks flying off of the faces of the people, off of the Bible and off of the floor and shooting through the air. Why is this happening?

We are at the River Chebar, so to speak. The water is augmenting, rising, getting deeper and wider. This river is full of the majesty of the Lord. In these risen waters, He is dressing us magnificently. His voice is upon these waters, and He is thundering against our enemies. And as His voice goes forth, it splits and flashes like forked lightning, releasing revelation. It is in the midst of these glorious waters that we now stand.

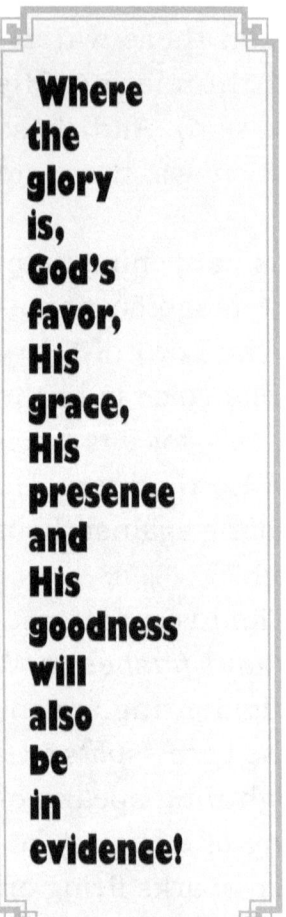

Where the glory is, God's favor, His grace, His presence and His goodness will also be in evidence!

Glorious Waters

Since these risen, augmenting rivers are glorious waters (according to the *Strong's* definition that we have already seen), they are obviously waters that are filled with the glory. And where the glory is, God's favor, His grace, His presence and His goodness will also be in evidence.

When Moses spoke face-to-face with the Lord, he said, *"If I have found favor in Your sight, show me now Your way"* (Exodus 33:13).

God answered, *"My Presence shall go with you"* (Verse 14).

Moses said, *"Show me Your glory"* (Verse 18).

The Lord answered, *"I will make all My goodness pass before you"* (Verse 19).

We cannot separate the glory from God's favor, His grace, His presence and His goodness, and neither could Moses.

The glory of God is so multifaceted. We have only begun to experience the streams of it. They are beginning to augment, and there will be rivers of the glory to swim in in the days ahead!

Triumphant Waters

These risen waters that are augmenting into a river to swim in are waters of triumph. Waters of triumph are waters full of great victories. These are victories that are complete and carry with them tremendous joy.

The word *triumph* comes from a victory pageant in which a general who had won a great victory over his enemies was paraded through the city streets. He was clothed in beautiful garments of gold. Behind the triumphant general in this great procession, chained to his chariot or to his horses, were his enemies. They followed behind him, shouting out insults about his weaknesses, failures and shortcomings. At the same time they were shouting out these accusations, others were throwing the petals of roses and other sweet-smelling flowers into the air, releasing their most beautiful fragrances.

With such a procession in mind, the apostle Paul wrote:

But thanks be to God, Who in Christ always leads us in TRIUMPH [as trophies of Christ's victory] and through us spreads and makes evident the fragrance of the knowledge of God everywhere. For we are the sweet fragrance of Christ [which exhales] unto God, [discernible alike] among those who are being saved and among those who are perishing: To the latter it is an aroma [wafted] from death to death [a fatal odor, the smell of doom]; to the former it is an aroma from life to life [a vital fragrance, living and fresh]. And who is qualified (fit and sufficient) for these things? [Who is able for such a ministry? We?].

2 Corinthians 2:14-16, Emphasis Added

The Lord will always lead us in triumph and total victory. We are His trophies that He displays in a triumphant procession. Our enemy, the accuser of the brethren, will always bring railing accusations against us as he follows behind. Through these great victories, however, the fragrance of our God will be spread because we know Him. This fragrance can and will be detected by the saved, as well as the lost. To those who are lost, it may smell like doom and death. To those who are saved, it will be a living and life-giving fragrance.

Who Is Qualified?

Paul went on to ask, *"Who is able* [or qualified] *for such a ministry? We?"* And the answer is, "Of course." We are qualified through Christ and His work in us.

These waters of triumph bring total victory in every area of our lives. Whatever need is presented to the Lord in these augmented, triumphant waters—whether it be healing, deliverance or anointing—that need is met. In triumphant waters, all enemies are defeated, and the fragrance of the Lord comes as a seal of the triumphant victory into which Christ always leads us.

The waters have just begun to flow, and as we are camped at the River Chebar, so to speak, the place of seeing the glory (the same glory that Ezekiel saw as his destiny came upon him), the river will augment, grow, enlarge, become much greater and more powerful. The waters will rise, becoming majestic, glorious and triumphant. What an awesome day in which to be alive! These are days of awe and wonder!

By Ezekiel 47:5, as we have already seen, the waters had risen. They were now *"waters to swim in, a river that could not be passed over or through."* This word *"river,"* *Strong's* (#5158), besides all the standard meanings of a river, means "the shaft of a mine." And what is brought forth through the shaft of a mine? Gold, silver, diamonds, rubies and emeralds and the like. These are what God is giving us today as His seal.

Evangelistic Waters

According to Ezekiel 47:1-5, many things had transpired at the threshold of the temple. The Shekinah cloud of God's presence, the glory, worship and powerful manifestations took place in the temple and at the threshold of it. Even though all of that transpired there, the waters did not *fill* the Temple. They issued out *from* the Temple, and became deeper the further they got from the Temple.

These are evangelistic waters of anointing for the harvest. We will experience God's glory, the Shekinah and powerful manifestations in the temple (the place of His presence), but the waters must always issue out toward the world, toward the needy ones. The further we go out to reach the lost with this glory, releasing in the process a fresh zeal for God's people that will remind them of their destiny, the greater the anointing and the greater the waters will become—until at last they will be rivers to swim in! This is the manifestation of *The Glory of God Revealed.*

Lord,

We are at the place of seeing the glory, the River Chebar. This is an augmenting river that will not decrease, but only enlarge. The waters are rising into majestic, glorious, triumphant waters, with rivers to swim in and many great fish to catch. Give us the heart of the Father to bring in the harvest and take us deeper into these waters with You!

Chapter 13

An Increasing Glory

O LORD, I have heard thy speech, and was afraid: O LORD, revive thy work in the midst of the years, in the midst of the years make known; in wrath remember mercy. God came from Teman, and the Holy One from mount Paran. Selah. His glory covered the heavens, and the earth was full of his praise. And his brightness was as the light; he had horns coming out of his hand; and there was the hiding of his power.

Habakkuk 3:2-4, KJV

As we have seen, when the glory comes, or is released into our midst, it comes for many reasons. Habakkuk, the wild, enthusiastic prophet, had already received a vision of the knowledge of the glory of the Lord covering the earth as the waters cover the sea, and now he has petitioned the Lord to come with a revival. Times have not changed, and human nature is still the same today. It has always been in the times of captivity and in wilderness experiences that God's people cry out to Him to move on their behalf.

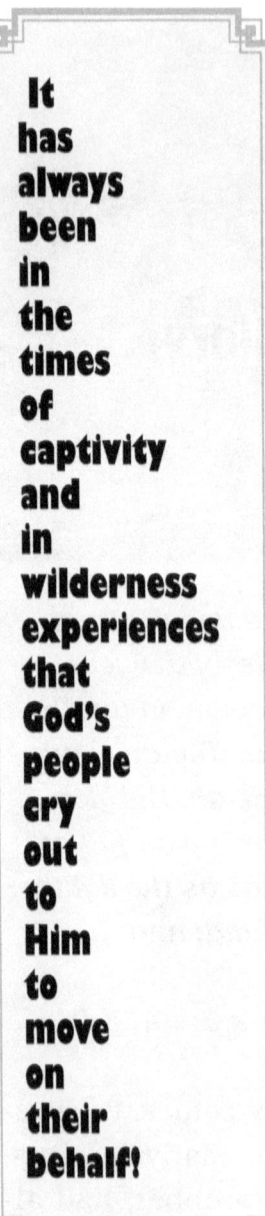

It has always been in the times of captivity and in wilderness experiences that God's people cry out to Him to move on their behalf!

Habakkuk cried out to the Lord to come and move as He had moved in other times, and immediately (in the very next verse), the King of Glory began to move. This was an immediate response to Habakkuk's prayer. And when the glory came as a result of Habakkuk's prayer, it came to bring increase, revival and the power of God.

Habakkuk wanted to see a move of God in the earth. He wanted God to bring a revival of those things that had been put in storage and hidden from His people. The Lord came to do it again in the days of a wild and enthusiastic prophet, and the

Lord is coming and doing it again in our day. Revival is upon us!

God came from Teman.   Habakkuk 3:3

According to *Strong's* (#8487), this word *"Teman"* means "the south," and *Strong's* (#3225), refers to a place of strength or the right hand." The word translated *"God"* here was *Elohim,* which means Creator. *Elohim* is plural, showing that God is more than one person. We serve the triune God—the great Three-in-One. Jesus is the Son of the right hand, and He is seated at the right hand of the Father in the place of power:

In the beginning [before all time] was the Word (Christ), and the Word was with God, and the Word was God Himself.
All things were made and came into existence through Him; and without Him was not even one thing made that has come into being.
                              John 1:1 and 3

The Bible leaves us with no doubts that Jesus is the only true and living God!

The Embellishing of the Lord

And the Holy One from Mount Paran.
                              Habakkuk 3:3

According to *Strong's* (#6290), *"Paran"* means "ornamental," and according to (#6286), "to gleam, embellish, beautify, glorify, glory." To *embellish* is "to make beautiful with ornamentation; to decorate; to heighten the attractiveness of by adding ornamental details; to adorn." The Holy One came from Mount Paran, the place of glory, but it was also the place of embellishing, beautifying and glorifying.

Once, when I was in a meeting at Calvary Pentecostal Campground in Ashland, Virginia, a pastor shared a testimony about something that happened when his wife was invited to minister to a group of women in India. Because she had understood that their custom was to wear no jewelry, she decided to dress down, so as not to offend them.

When she and her husband arrived at the meeting, they found that it was true that the women did not wear jewelry, but much to her surprise, the Indian ladies had on garments that were very ornately trimmed with gold and other beautiful colors. She left the room in tears, feeling that she was not properly dressed for the occasion.

In an adjoining room, her husband comforted her. "But I have dressed so poorly," she objected, and he could see her eyes brimming with tears. Then, suddenly, as they spoke, the glory of Heaven began to embellish her. A beautiful, gold, tinsel-like substance began to cover her clothes. Until that time, she and her husband had not heard of the various glory manifestations. They did not know that the

Lord was covering His people in gold dust. But even though they had never heard of what was happening with others, they knew that this was from the Lord. The Lord was decorating his wife, making her beautiful, adorning her, heightening her attractiveness by adding ornamental details.

His Glory Is Imposing

His glory covered the heavens. Habakkuk 3:3

"Glory," according to *Strong's* (#1935), means "majesty, grandeur (an imposing form and appearance): beauty, excellency." When something is *imposing, Webster's* describes it as "using superior strength or authority to secure submission to [one's will], to force others to receive [especially oneself] as guest or companion." The prophet cried for revival, and the Lord came in an imposing form and appearance. He came in with His glory, and those who were a part of that great visitation to the earth knew that He was God and that He had come to bring revival.

God had also come to secure their submission to His will. He came that they would receive Him as their guest and companion. Those who were in that day of great visitation from the Lord, just like today, could accept Him in His glory, or they could reject Him. But He came anyway, and there was no denying that He, the King of Glory, had come to visit the earth!

In this day of great visitation, the King of Glory is coming to reveal things that He has kept stored up for this hour. He is reviving us, but He is coming in a superior strength and authority, to secure our submission to His will for us, so that we will choose to fulfill His call upon our lives. We can have Him continually in our lives, moment by moment, every day, not only as guest, but as our eternal companion and friend.

The Glory Brings Fresh Anointing

"Covered," according to *Strong's* (#3680 and $3789) means "to cover, to blanket, to overwhelm, to plump, to fill up hollows, to grow fat." *"Heavens,"* according to *Strong's* (#8064), means "to be lofty; the sky: air." God's glory, His majesty and grandeur, in an imposing form and appearance, came and began to cover, to blanket and to overwhelm the air and the sky, and to make the very atmosphere plumped up and fat. In other words, His glory came in a visible, manifested form. As it covered the air, the atmosphere and the sky, it brought forth the anointing. To *plump up* or to *make fat,* then, means "to anoint."

Just as the glory covered, or blanketed, the air, it filled up the hollow parts. Hollow parts are parts that are empty or void of what they need. A hollow can also represent a space to be filled, in this case to contain power. Many times our space for containing the power of God becomes hollow. At times, our spirit man, or heart, that once was on fire for the Lord and filled up with the power of the Holy Spirit, becomes dried and shriveled up. Our place of power is not what it used to be. We have allowed ourselves to become empty and void of the Holy Spirit flowing in our lives. Then, when the glory comes and begins to cover the air or the atmosphere, it begins to fill up all the empty places that have become void of the power of God. That is why hearts are revived when the glory comes!

Many times our space for containing the power of God becomes hollow!

The Earth Is Filled with the Glory of the Lord

And the earth was full of His praise.   Habakkuk 3:3

"Earth," according to *Strong's* (#776), means "field, ground, land, wilderness." *"Praise,"* according to *Strong's* (#8416 and #1984), means "to be clear (originally of sound, but usually of color); to shine; to give in marriage." The earth, the ground, the wilderness, the land and the field were filled with God's praise.

We usually think of praise in terms of sound, but here we see that it can also refer to color. As we have discussed before, it is our praise and our worship to the Lord that releases the realms of His glory, and often the result is a display of color. Our praise and adoration to God brings an atmosphere charged with the supernatural realms of Heaven. Many of the resulting manifestations appear in diverse colors, and they are also sometimes clear in appearance, such as crystalline or diamond dust.

We must remember that when the Lord is dressing His Bride and He decks her in gold and silver, it is because she is being taken in marriage. *Praise* here also means "to be given in marriage." The earth and the wilderness were filled with God's praise, and the earth and the wilderness were given in marriage. As the earth and the wilderness were filled with His praise, it brought forth a shining.

He Is Light

And His brightness was like the sunlight.
Habakkuk 3:4

"Brightness," according to *Strong's* (#5050 and 5051), means "brilliancy, light, clear shining, glitter." In the Lord's brightness and brilliancy, His light, His clear shining, His glitter, was like the sunlight, or as the King James Version translates it, was *"like the light."*

This word *"light,"* according to *Strong's* (#216 and #215), has the same meaning as *"shine"* in Isaiah 60:1, where the Lord said, *"Arise! Shine!"* The meanings are "illumination, luminary, lightning, happiness, to make luminous (literally and metaphorically), break of day, glorious, set on fire."

As I stated in Chapter 4, in the phrase, "Arise and Shine," the word *shine,* according to the *Webster's,* means "sparkle" and "glitter." The Lord's brightness was like illumination. It was like a luminary that shines upon us. His brightness was like lightning.

As noted earlier, the word *"lightning"* in the Word of God speaks of revelation. The Lord's brightness is revelation to us. His brightness is happiness. It makes us luminous—literally and metaphorically. His brightness is as the break of day. It is glorious. It sets us on fire!

God's brightness, His brilliancy, His clear shining, His glitter, is illumination to us. As we have already seen, the glory brings revelation. God's brilliancy, His clear shining, His glitter, is our luminary, shining upon us. His brilliancy, His clear shining, His glitter, is lightning, or revelation, to us. His brilliancy, His clear shining, His glitter, is happiness to us, and it causes us to be luminous—literally as well as metaphorically.

He Is the Source of All Power

He had horns coming out of his hand.
Habakkuk 3:4, KJV

Habakkuk saw the Lord with horns coming out of His hand. This word *"horns,"* according to *Strong's* (#7161), has many meanings. Two of them are: "a ray of light" and "power." The Lord had horns—rays of light and power—coming out of His hand. This is the same manifestation that took place with Moses on Mount Sinai:

When we step into the realms of God's glory, we experience the marvels and wonders of the Lord!

When Moses came down from Mount Sinai with the two tables of the Testimony in his hand, he did not know that the skin of his face shone and sent forth beams by reason of his speaking with the Lord.
                                    Exodus 34:29

Upon Moses' face, there was a splendor, and it caused his face to shine as if light was coming from it. These rays that came from Moses' face were a result of his having been in the presence of the Lord and experiencing the glory of the Lord for forty days.

This word *"hand,"* according to *Strong's* (#3027), means "the place of power." Rays of light and power came from the place of power.

In His Glory Is His Power

And there [in the sunlike splendor] was the hiding place of His power. Habakkuk 3:4

In the midst of God's glory, His brilliance, His shining, His illumination and His *"sunlike splendor"* as rays of light coming from His hand, was the hiding place of His power. I believe this is the reason that when we step into the realms of God's glory, or He allows us to go into the dwelling places of His glory, we experience the marvels and wonders of the Lord. We experience His power—His miracle-working power. We cannot heal or deliver anyone, but He is the Deliverer and Healer, and when we get into His glory, miracles just happen!

His Glory and His Presence Will Dwell with Us

Surely His salvation is near to those who reverently and worshipfully fear Him, [and is ready to be appropriated] that [the manifest presence of God, His] glory may tabernacle and abide in our land. Psalm 85:9

This scripture says it all! God's salvation encompasses so much. It includes His saving grace for eternal life, His saving us from sickness, His saving us from death, His saving us from perilous times and His saving us from attacks. We are being saved daily! All that we need is near us when we fear and worship Him.

Because of this, we can learn to appropriate God's manifested presence, His glory, and when we do, it can then tabernacle with us. All we have to do is be willing, and we can pitch our tent, so to speak, or tabernacle with or dwell with our God, in His dwelling places forever. What could be more important than *The Glory of God Revealed?*

Father,

We have asked for revival and for Your glory, and You are coming and doing it in this hour. Father, help us not to miss the day of Your great visitation, of Your glory and Your power! Come with Your manifested presence, which is Your glory, and pitch Your tent in our land and abide with us!

Chapter 14

From Glory to Glory

Now the Lord is the Spirit, and where the Spirit of the Lord is, there is liberty (emancipation from bondage, freedom). And all of us, as with unveiled face, [because we] continued to behold [in the Word of God] as in a mirror the glory of the Lord, are constantly being transfigured into His very own image in ever increasing splendor and from one degree of glory to another; [for this comes] from the Lord [Who is] the Spirit.

2 Corinthians 3:17-18

As we, with unveiled faces, continue to behold in the Word of God [Jesus], as in a mirror, the glory of the Lord, we are constantly being transfigured into His image in ever increasing splendor. What does this mean?

As we are beholding Jesus, who is the Word of God, with faces no longer covered by a veil, but are now face-to-face with Him, we are constantly becoming more and more like Him. As we gaze upon Him through this mirror and we are changed into His likeness, we are literally being transfigured into His image. As we gaze upon Him, the Word of God, the glory that is upon Him is then placed upon us.

There is no longer a veil that prevents us from seeing Him, but we see Him face-to-face. And all that He is begins to come upon us. From one degree, or realm of glory, to another realm of glory, we are being changed into the likeness of the Word of God. The key here is the phrase *face-to-face*.

We saw in the first chapter, "The Glory," that it was because Moses sought God's face that the Lord showed him His glory. The glory does not come hand-to-face, or hand-to-hand, but face-to-face. This is because the glory is the Lord's manifested presence.

We saw in Chapter 13, "An Increasing Glory," that the Lord's manifested presence was His glory and that it can tabernacle with us. This word *presence* means "the turning of the face." The Lord's presence is coming to us in such a way that we are suddenly face-to-face with Him. He is turning His face toward us.

As He turns towards us, and we are beholding Him face-to-face, as in a mirror, we are being changed from one realm of glory to another realm of glory.

From Glory to Glory

There are many realms of God's glory. Some of them cannot be felt or seen, while others are visible and tangible. Some realms of His glory are felt only deep within our souls or inside our physical bodies. Each realm of His glory comes to change us into His likeness.

Is one realm of the glory more important than another? No! All are needed. I do believe, however, that in this hour of the glory being poured out upon the earth, we may step out of some of the former glories into newer realms of glory. There are former glories that we have experienced, but there are latter glories that yet await us.

The manifestation of God's glory is intensifying. I like the way the King James Bible expresses it:

Now the Lord is that Spirit: and where the Spirit of the Lord is, there is liberty. But

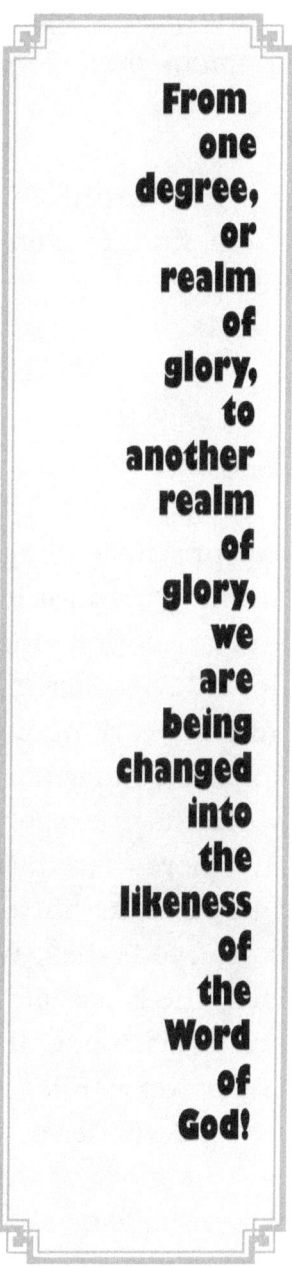

From one degree, or realm of glory, to another realm of glory, we are being changed into the likeness of the Word of God!

we all, with open face beholding as in a glass the glory of the Lord, are changed into the same image from glory to glory.

2 Corinthians 3:17-18, KJV

The Amplified Bible translates this phrase *"from glory to glory"* as *"from one degree of glory to another."*

A Catapulting Effect

When we are in the glory, it has a catapulting effect upon our lives. As you have seen throughout the previous chapters, the glory dresses us and marks us, and it looses destiny and releases revival and revelation upon us. It also touches the unbeliever. The glory charges the atmosphere with the miracle-working power of God, and when this atmospheric change comes, healings take place, financial problems are resolved and lives are transformed.

Where there has been sickness or pain, the glory catapults us out of sickness and pain into healed, pain-free bodies. Where there has been poverty and lack, the glory catapults us to new levels of blessings and provision. Our lives are changed in every way as His power is released.

This wonderful and awesome atmosphere of Heaven, the glory of God, the anointing that breaks the yoke, releases change. When we are in the realms of God's glory, the change in us is so great that we are catapulted to new levels in Him. We suddenly step into new levels of understanding, new levels of revelation, new levels of anointing and new levels of passion for Him.

When His glory comes to change us, that change is dramatic, and we are never the same again. We are catapulted out of our present standing, and we suddenly break through into things for which we have been seeking the Lord—sometimes for a very long time.

In this current great visitation from the Lord, He is releasing wondrous new realms of His glory. The former rain and its former glories have been seen and partaken of. Now, the latter rain with its fresh glories is coming.

None of us has, as yet, comprehended the totality of what the Lord has in store for us, but we do know that it will be grand. We serve a God of great progression. He wants to move us forward, changing us and thrusting us to new levels of His anointing and glory. He wants to fulfill our destinies!

His plan is a big one, and what He does for you will affect not only you, but everyone else around you. What He does for you may even affect entire nations! That is the result of *The Glory of God Revealed.*

Lord,

It is from glory to glory that we are being changed into Your image! As You release more of Your glory upon us, we are becoming more like You! Your glory has a transforming power that can catapult us to new levels in You! Lord, change us from one realm of Your glory to another. Transform us and thrust us into Your plans and purposes for our lives!

Testimonies of the Glory

"My wife and I were invited to a meeting in Slidell, Louisiana. At the time, I was working in Mobile, Alabama, a hundred miles from home.

"Even though I am a Full Gospel minister, I had some reservations about the gold dust. I had read and heard about it, but wasn't sure of the reasoning behind it. So when we went to the meeting in Slidell, my wife didn't tell me that it was to be a teaching on the glory and its manifestations here on earth. She also didn't tell me that these people were experiencing gold dust falling in their meetings. I learned that only after we had arrived and were on our way into the meeting.

"I told God that I didn't need to see gold fall to believe Him for healing and miracles. I had been exposed to many healings through the years and also the miracle of God filling teeth, but I was in for a big surprise.

"Sister Andy started the service, and throughout the song service and preaching, my wife kept seeing sparks of gold shooting out into the air. Then, when Sister Andy began laying hands on people and praying for them, gold dust suddenly appeared on plants and tables and on the people who were being prayed for. The gold would form in the air and then just fall as if it came from Heaven—which, obviously, it did.

"One woman who was prayed for was covered from head to toe in a mixture of beautiful green and blue dust, and somehow it matched the outfit she was wearing. Almost every person had gold dust on them.

"I wasn't against what was happening, but I wasn't anxious for it to happen to me. I went to the rest room, hoping to avoid being prayed for. While I was there, I washed my face, using the mirror. For some reason, I felt that I should look in my mouth, and when I did, I found that all of my fillings had turned to a very bright, shiny platinum color. And I had not even been prayed for yet.

"We left the meeting to drive the hundred miles home, and we talked about the meeting all the way home. After we got home, my wife was tired and went to bed, but I kept looking at my teeth. I went to get some dental floss from my wife's purse to check my teeth out further and discovered that inside of her purse was blue and green dust on everything, including her wallet and her checkbook.

"Suddenly, I got the urge to look at her teeth. By this time she had gotten out of the bed and was looking through everything in her purse. We were both amazed. We were further amazed to find that she had gold fillings, one in the shape of a cross and another with a jewel embedded in it. The next day we had gold dust on our hands all day.

"That Monday night we went to my sister's café, where they were having prayer meetings, and we shared with them what had transpired. Everyone got gold dust on their hands, face and clothes. We had teeth filled, along with the manifestation of crystals and jade flakes falling. People were on their hands and knees looking for gold.

"Every day after that there was something new. I went to my dentist, and he and his staff wouldn't say that my teeth were gold or platinum, but they kept asking what I had used to get such a high shine on my previously dark fillings. I told them I had been in a meeting where God had changed my fillings from dark fillings to the bright, shiny ones that they were looking at. They agreed with me, and let it go at that.

"God has been doing many wonderful things since that time. Although we are moving on in ministry, we are asking God every day, 'What next, Lord?' We thank the Lord for bringing this anointed sister into our lives."

Rev. Sam and Billie Meeks
Picayune, Mississippi

"Sister Andy ministered in our 'Ushering in God's Glory' revival meetings, and here are some testimonies of what took place as a result of her ministry:

"Jeffery, a young boy with a learning disability and stomach problems, was healed. He is functioning normally now and getting A's in school. His stomach problems are gone, and his mother is amazed.

"Patricia was healed of cancer, and her mother is out of her wheelchair and off of oxygen.

"Bruce Freshwater took his daughter who had heart problems to the doctor, and he did an EKG on her. The doctors were amazed at the changes in her heart!

"One lady had oil appearing on the finger that Sister Andy prayed for and is being healed daily of agonizing, throbbing pain. She is amazed!

"Marian has had more gold dust appear on her while listening to Sister Andy's tapes.

"Many of the prophecies Andy spoke over people's lives have already begun to come to pass.

"There were also many gold fillings, and the fragrance of the Lord was all over the church.

"New testimonies continue to roll in. The impartation continues to grow. New people are coming into the ministry, and gold dust is manifesting on the people and their houses."

Pastor Jim Boley
Healing Waters Church
Charleston, South Carolina

᪣

"I began attending Sister Andy's meetings in November of 1998. Shortly after we entered into the year 2000, we spiritually stepped into a new dimension in the Lord. We have come to call this new move 'the Glory Revival.' Since then, we have been experiencing the glory in gold dust and other manifestations in every meeting. A few months after it began, I, too, started experiencing gold dust on my hands and arms. Not long afterward, after worshiping the Lord in my home one day, I got into my car and discovered gold dust on my pants and also on the inside of my car.

"On Good Friday, April 21, 2000, I was on the telephone praying with a friend from church. We were in the midst of our intercession when I remembered that I had left the sprinkler on outside. I went outside to turn off the sprinkler, and my eye caught a glimpse of something glistening on the side of our house. When I looked closer, I realized that there was silver dust all over the front of our home.

"I proceeded to walk up our front steps onto the porch, and I could see that the silver dust was all over the railings, the porch and the steps. I then spotted the silver dust in the dirt in front of the house. I walked all over the property, which is a little over an acre, and I found the silver everywhere there was no grass. As I write this testimony (July of 2000), we still have silver dust all over the outside of our house and in the dirt. God is so magnificent!

"One day after taking a shower, I had gold dust all over my legs. I have had gold dust on my clothing after our Wednesday worship and teaching meetings with Andy, and I have had gold dust on myself after worshiping in my home. Even after I've washed my clothes or sent them to the cleaners, the gold dust will still remain in my clothing. After many months, the gold and silver dust has still remained in my car and on our home. I also have it on some of my shoes and on my Bible cover. Praise the Lord!"

Cheryl Dunn
Mandeville, Louisiana

&

"My first experience with the golden glory happened in January of 2000. Andy had just returned from a conference at Sister Ruth Ward Heflin's campground in Virginia. We drove down to New Orleans to an Aglow meeting where Andy was speaking. She talked about the glory that night, and as people came forward for prayer afterward, we began to see flecks of gold dust on their faces and clothes.

"I was quite surprised by this, even though I had heard of this manifestation. You could say that I was a little skeptical or, as some came to call me, 'a doubting Thomas.' As we drove home that night, I looked down at my skirt and noticed something glittering. I called Andy's attention to my glittering skirt, and she had no doubt at all that it was God's glory being manifested before our very eyes.

"The logical side of my brain wanted to try to explain the whole thing away. Maybe the glitter was part of the fabric. All the way home I teetered somewhere between doubt and amazement.

"When I was getting undressed that evening, I decided to try a little experiment to put my mind at rest about all of this. I laid a blouse on the counter in the bathroom and then took off my skirt and proceeded to shake it onto the blouse. To my surprise and delight, tiny gold flakes fell onto the blouse. With that, my theory about the glitter being somehow in the fabric vanished, and thus began a year of signs and wonders. And I was as amazed as anyone else by it all.

"In some meetings, Andy was asked not to speak about the gold dust, so when the people would come down for prayer, she and I would look at each other and smile. We could see the glory forming on the people's faces and clothes.

"Many times since then, when I was least expecting it, I would see a speck here or there, and the thought would come to me that my God was saying, 'I'm here.' This gave me the feeling that He was taking delight in showing Himself in this way.

"Once, when we were doing some meetings in a church in Lafayette, we went back to the hotel one night after the meeting and went to our rooms. I wanted to sit down on the bed and eat some tacos I had bought on the way, and when I went to pull back the bedspread, I saw that it was covered with gold dust. I was so excited that I ran to Andy's room and had her come and see. It was beautiful and so much fun. The Lord delights in surprising His children.

"During that first week of seeing God's glory, another unusual thing happened to me. I was driving to an appointment one day, and while I was stopped at a traffic light, I was rummaging through my purse, looking for something. To my surprise, I pulled out a small, round, crystal-like bead. My thought was, *What is this? And where did it come from?* Then I dropped it and couldn't find it again, so I didn't think about it anymore.

"Later that week, Andy was teaching in Prairieville, and during the meeting someone came up to me and said that there were small round crystal-looking things all over the floor and on the pews. When I saw them, immediately my mind went racing back to the day in the car. This was the same thing I had found in my purse.

"That night we found crystals all over the church, and they had not been there when we arrived. Someone always swept the floors before the meetings. The next week, Andy took the crystals to a jeweler, who confirmed that they were pure crystal. While she was there, the same type of crystals began to appear all over the floor of the jeweler's home. His wife and children had gold dust on them too. God is so amazing!

"There have been many more times of experiencing God's glory in wonderful ways. I have seen oil coming from people's hands, puddles of golden oil on church pews, gold, green and blue flakes on clothes, faces, hands and hair, and even a golden sky in Israel. My life has been changed by all of this, and the desire to see God's glory cover the whole earth is with me every day. I believe that we truly cannot comprehend the things to come and the awesome ways that a living God desires to reveal Himself."

Cindy Stevens
Baton Rouge, Louisiana

ও

"I first experienced the manifestation of God's golden glory when I was on the way to a meeting, in New Orleans, Louisiana, at which Sister Andy (my mom) would be ministering. She had just returned from Sister Ruth's camp in Ashland, Virginia, and had received a greater impartation of the glory. As we were worshiping together in the car, Mom was calling forth the manifested presence of God and, sure enough, it came.

"I looked down at my hands, and they were covered in a clear, shiny substance, which I later found out was crystal. This happened at the beginning of January of 2000, and it is still manifesting to this very day (August 7, 2000). Gold dust covers my hands, face and neck, and it is there almost every day since the Lord began showing us His glory.

"Seeing the presence of God like this has totally changed my life and increased my faith. Just one week of being in His glory, which brings a super-natural anointing and atmosphere, gave me a whole new passion for serving the Lord. The glory is now starting to appear on my friends at church while I'm talking to them. It's incredible!

"In April we went to Israel, and while having communion on the Sea of Galilee, we were all covered with gold dust. As we walked on the land of Israel, our feet began to be covered in gold dust and dust of other colors.

"Through the impartation of this manifestation from my mother, I have also received a greater understanding of the Word of God. Great revelations have come. God is still removing the 'onion skins' from my eyes every time I am in His presence. I cannot wait for the whole world to know about this awesome God we serve and to see Him in all His glory."

Elizabeth "Lizzie" Blythe
Expressions Youth Leader
Baton Rouge, Louisiana

"God is an awesome God. The first time I went to one of Sister Andy's services, I was covered in gold dust. It was all over my black pantsuit. The second meeting I was in, my hands were covered in gold dust. The third time I went, crystals began to appear as we were worshiping, and there was a crystal on the floor in front of me.

"I bought one of Andy's tapes and played it in my truck, and red, gold, blue and green dust began to appear all over the dashboard.

"I have been attending Andy's services since January 2000, and God is still moving there. In every meeting there is a manifestation of the glory, with people getting gold dust on them or gold fillings in their teeth."

Gayle Bates
Prairieville, Louisiana

"In January of 2000, I went to one of Sister Andy's meetings. At the end of the meeting, I saw that I had gold dust all over my hands—as did everyone else there. It then began to appear on my clothes and personal belongings. Every time we are in one of Andy's meetings, it appears on us.

"When I went to Israel with her group, I discovered it on my feet. It kept appearing and still does today. I have seen gold, crystalline, ruby, emerald and silver dust as well.

"About six months after I first received the gold dust, oil began coming through the pores of my hands and feet. My life will never be the same and has been so exciting since experiencing God's golden glory."

Amanda Lee
Baton Rouge, Louisiana

"Recently I started to attend Sister Andy's ministry meetings at a local church. There were people there receiving gold dust and gold fillings. On my second visit, Andy recommended that we read the book *Golden Glory* by Ruth Ward Heflin. The book contains many testimonies about the gold manifestations now happening around the world.

"Because of my granddaughter's illness, I put the book aside and forgot about it. About two weeks later, I came across the book and read four or five chapters before leaving home for the day. Later that evening, as I was brushing my teeth, I saw something shining in my mouth. Calling to my husband in the living room, I asked him to come look. He saw that an old silver crown, which had turned black on one side a few years before, was now completely gold.

"It was not just gold; it was a brilliant gold, and my husband was so excited that he had to tell someone. We remembered a friend at another church who had a similar experience, a filling turning gold, and my husband called him. While he was on the phone, he asked me to open my mouth so that he could see my tooth again. In those few minutes since the first crown had turned gold, two more crowns had turned gold. These were not of the brilliant gold, like the first one, but of a low-luster gold. Later that evening, the filling in another tooth turned gold.

"By this time, my husband was so excited that he kept going to the mirror to check his own teeth, to see if any of them had turned gold. None of them had. That night he talked to God and asked Him why he had not received a similar miracle. The Lord reminded him that it had been my birthday and said that this was His gift to me. Since my earthly father had never remembered my birthday, my heavenly Father had.

"Some people have chosen to ignore what God is doing, and others still refuse to believe that this is from God. Someone very close to me said he considered my miracle to be vulgar and wished I had never received it. To me, however, the gold teeth are indeed a most precious gift from my heavenly Father."

Susan Lachney
Covington, Louisiana

୶

"The first time I attended a meeting with Sister Andy I had just recently heard about the 'gold dust' manifestation and was really struggling with it. I attended the meeting full of questions, my mind wrestling with unbelief.

"At the close of the service, Andy asked for all of the pastors to come forward to receive an impartation. Although I was very reluctant, I felt the nudging of the Holy Spirit to go to the front. When it came my turn to be ministered to, She asked me if I was a writer and if I had ever written any books. I affirmed that both were true. Andy then told me that she saw me writing another book and told me several other things that were very meaningful and real in my life.

"When Andy prayed for me, I felt a very weighty anointing of the Holy Spirit. It was so heavy upon me that I could not move for a while. As I basked in the presence of the Lord, all of my doubts and fears about the gold dust vanished. It was an unforgettable experience.

"Soon after that, my husband and I were able to attend a meeting with Sister Andy together. We were very blessed with the meeting, but an even greater blessing came when we went to open up the church doors for our own service the following Sunday. There was a sprinkling of gold dust on the artificial trees on our platform. That gold dust remains there to this day.

"The entire gold dust manifestation has brought a fresh sense of awe and wonder to us and our people, and we have received a great refreshing as a result through Sister Andy's ministry. The greatest joy has been to minister this to others."

Pastor Sharon Vincent
Abba Church
Lafayette, Louisiana

ॐ

"We invited Sister Andy to minister to us on the glory. I had been having an annoying pain and discomfort in my lower back for several months. I knew the Word of God, and I believed in His healing power, I prayed the healing Scriptures, and I stood on His Word, but for some reason, my healing had not come.

"While we were in praise and worship, I felt a tingling in my body from my head down toward my lower back. I was joyful, knowing that we were before the throne of God, and He was doing a miracle in me. At that time, I didn't know exactly what He was doing. I just knew that it would be good.

"After praise and worship, Sister Andy said that God was moving and healing people and asked that anyone who needed a healing come forward. I went up to let her lay hands on me and pray. God completed my healing, as I felt the tingling go down to my feet. Under the love of God, I couldn't move for five full minutes. Now, I am completely healed. Thank You, Lord Jesus!

"We also had gold dust and gold fillings begin to manifest as Sister Andy was teaching. The children had different colors all over their faces and their clothing. Everyone that night received an impartation of gold dust."

Robert Avery
Lafayette, Louisiana

᷾

"In January of 1998, I rededicated my life to the Lord. This time, I was not just saved, but I was completely in love with the Lord. Shortly after this, I went to a women's retreat where Sister Ruth Ward Heflin was ministering in Pass Christian, Mississippi. It was the first time I had come in contact with the gold dust.

"At the close of one of the meetings, Sister Ruth prayed over us to receive an impartation of the gold dust. I would see it on me during the meetings.

"In 1999, I began to be involved in Sister Andy's meetings in the Prairieville area, and in January of 2000, the Lord began to pour out His glory upon us in those meetings. A new impartation came to me, and I began to see the gold dust and many other colors of particles on me and in my home on a daily basis.

"During that first meeting in Prairieville, when the gold dust fell like rain, we were literally covered in a dusting of gold and other colors. It was incredible to us that, as we worshiped Him, He would pour out such a beautiful display of His glory upon us. Puddles of golden oil formed on the church pews, and gold dust all over the pulpit and Sister Andy's Bible.

"The next week, we were praising and worshiping, and the gold dust began to manifest, as it had the week before. This time, before we were finished singing, people began to see smooth, round stones appearing all over the floor. There were many of them, and people began picking them up.

"As we continued to worship the Lord, I noticed that instead of gold dust on my clothes, this time there was what appeared to be a shredded, fine glass forming all over my clothes. I continued dancing before the Lord, and I held my skirt up a little so that the strange substance could accumulate there.

"When the people were picking up the stones, I had not wanted to break my worship to get one, so I told the Lord that if He wanted me to have one, He would have to give it to me in His own way. All I wanted was to worship Him!

"Then, suddenly, I began to feel something underneath my foot, and I had an urge to see what it was. I picked it up and found that it was like the smooth, round stones that had appeared earlier in the meeting. This one did not seem to be completely formed. It was later examined by a jeweler, and he said that it was indeed a crystal that was not completely formed.

"Since the release of the Lord's glory in those meetings, I have gold dust or other colors on me every day. It forms in my home in the places that I pray or study my Bible. Experiencing the Lord's glory has placed a fire in my life that cannot be quenched. All I want to do is to pray and worship Him. This is not to receive anything, but just because I love Him!"

Tonya Slay
Walker, Louisiana

❧

"My life has been changed since I became part of Sister Andy's ministry. God has done such a positive work in my life and in the lives of my family members as well. From the moment I began worshiping the Lord with the group and sat under Andy's teaching, my life was stirred to be all that I could be for God.

I began to worship the Lord with greater excitement and expectation, and the presence of God became very real when I praised Him. Suddenly, I knew that all things were possible, and my faith was stirred and increased to believe for greater miracles.

"Andy's teaching is very exciting, for God continues to give her revelation knowledge on the Word of God that is life-changing. It has challenged me to dive into the Word of God, spending more and more time alone with my Savior, Jesus Christ, and learning to abide in Him moment by moment. I am still changing, and I love the things the Lord is doing in my life.

"I have been in Andy's ministry since it began and have witnessed powerful miracles from God. She flows in the gift of prophecy, and she will pray over people for hours and minister to them with all of her heart, many times receiving a word of prophecy for each person. My daughter Amy and I have had the privilege of traveling with Andy for meetings and conferences. This has enabled us to witness firsthand the precious anointing of God upon her life and how she gives one hundred percent of herself to minister to others.

"God began to do a mighty work in our family life as we applied the things we were being taught every week. We experienced a new unity, less friction with everyday life and more peace than we had ever known. We all now have more love for one another, less impatience and more kindness and thoughtfulness.

"We have witnessed many miracles in Andy's meetings—the gold dust and gold fillings among them. This had never been her focus, but rather a manifestation of God's presence many times as we have worshiped the Lord. It is hard not to get excited when you see gold dust on you or on the person next to you! Most of the time it appears on our faces, arms and hands, but we have seen it just about everywhere.

"Amy and I began to see it in our home almost daily. This increased our faith for greater things and made us feel very special, that the Lord would pour down His gold for us in these latter days. We have witnessed it in many different cities as we have traveled with Andy. We have also seen firsthand many gold fillings take place. We saw the teeth before she prayed, and then again afterwards, and they would be very different. It was just amazing!

"This is only the beginning of what God has been doing in our midst. I have personally seen blind and damaged eyes healed, severely damaged backs healed, cancer healed, relationships healed, and every type of sickness and diseases healed. Indeed, our God is no respecter of persons.

"In all of this, Andy is very careful to give all the glory to God for these miracles, for she knows she is simply the servant He has chosen to use. But she is willing to be used to bring forth the glory of God.

"It has been such an honor to be Andy's friend and part of her ministry. This has enabled me to draw closer to my Lord and Savior. It has opened my eyes to God's Word as never before. I have a new revelation of God and what He wants for my life.

"I watched Amy change profoundly as she started attending Andy's meetings. She is just seventeen, but she is completely sold out for God and wants to be used for Him in every way possible. She has a brighter countenance now and is filled with God's love and His joy.

"Everyone I know who has been involved with this ministry has been changed. God is so good to have brought into our midst someone as awesome as Andy. We thank God for her and all that she is teaching us. She is one amazing woman of God, and we love her so much!"

Melanie Saines
formerly of Mandeville, Louisiana,
now of Houston, Texas

I must add a few lines of testimony here myself:

Concerning Pastors Wilfred and Addie Scott of Rhema Christian Center in Baker, Louisiana:

I first met Pastor Scott and his wife Addie in New Orleans at the Christian Booksellers' Association Conference where Sister Ruth Ward Heflin was ministering, along with Bob Shattles and David Herzog. Soon after that meeting, I was invited to their church to minister. Before I spoke for them, however, they came to a meeting where I was ministering at the Church of Acts in Lafayette, Louisiana. Before Pastor Addie ever came down front for prayer, she was already covered with many beautiful colors of glitter, particularly green and red.

When I did go to their church to minister, many received an impartation of the glory the Lord was displaying. It began to manifest on the chairs and the platform. When I went back a second time, many of their people reported that it was now in their homes and their cars and also upon their children. At that second meeting, not just gold dust appeared, but also crystals and cut stones.

Concerning Meadowood Methodist Church in Prairieville, Louisiana:

In our meetings there, gold dust poured on us like rain. A visible golden cloud formed in the sanctuary. People said they were sitting in gold dust. Gold dust covered the pulpit and my Bible. It was all over the altar, and there were puddles of golden oil on the pews as well. An impartation came to the people as I would lay hands on them. Gold fillings began to appear during the preaching of the Word of God and during the laying on of hands. Golden sparks flew off of the people's faces and through the air. When the people would go home and undress, there was much more

243

gold under their garments than on them. It was also on their purses, wallets and on the pages of their Bibles.

The next week there was more of the same, but this time pure crystals appeared as we worshiped—probably a hundred or more of them. These were examined by jewelers and were found to be of the purest form of crystal. One jeweler said that if you could cluster them together, they would form either gold or blue topazes. We later learned that these crystals fit the description of what Ezekiel saw in his visions of the glory. One of these crystals, a jeweler later confirmed, turned into an alexandrite. The cloud of God's presence was literally seen in those meetings.

Concerning the State Women's Conference of Aglow International in Pass Christian, Mississippi:

Many of the women present were covered with golden dust and with flakes in many other colors. Some said that they could see it falling like rain over the meetings. Bible pages were covered in gold dust. One lady had so much gold appearing on her Bible that others were approaching her and shaking the golden flakes off onto their Bibles. The gold seemed not to run out. A cloud of God's presence also appeared and was seen by many.

Concerning Sue Avery of Lafayette, Louisiana:

I was invited by Sue and her husband Robert to come to Lafayette and minister on the glory. There were other ministers and pastors in the meeting. During the preaching of the Word of God, gold dust began to manifest on the people where they were sitting. Pastor Ron Breaux was the first to come down front that evening and receive an impartation of gold dust. Before the evening was over, everyone had gold dust and other colored dust all over them—some on their hands, others on their faces and clothes. The children were literally covered. It was on their faces, clothes and hands. People also received gold fillings. In Sue's home, gold dust literally became embedded into the floor where she stood to make coffee.

Concerning Pastors Harold and Sharon Vincent of Abba Church in Lafayette, Louisiana:

It was such a joy to be able to minister in Pastors Harold and Sharon's church for two glory conferences. Both times the impartation was very powerful. The glory was poured out in such a marvelous way upon the people, but especially upon the children. The testimonies that came later of the increasing glory upon the people were truly a blessing. When the impartation goes forth, it increases and multiplies!

There was a wonderful realm of the glory that visited us in those meetings, and many healings manifested. Each time I ministered during those meetings, the glory anointing increased upon my life. Toward the end of the meetings, I was waking up to find my bed full of gold dust and my hands looking as if they were painted gold and silver.

On our way back home, whenever we got out of the car, gold dust and other colored particles would appear on the seat of the car. I stopped to visit my mother and sister who had come to the meetings to hear me minister, but had left early because the prayer lines were so long. They were saddened because they had not seen the gold dust on them during the meetings. I prayed for them, and gold dust begin to manifest on both of them.

I prayed for my sister to receive fillings, and then we left to get back to Baton Rouge. After we were back on the highway, I got a phone call from my mother. She wanted us to come back and see what God had done. Even though I had not laid hands on her for gold fillings, the Lord had given here a big beautiful gold crown

❧

In all of these meetings, there were many people giving their lives to the Lord and many being filled with the Holy Spirit, common fruits of the manifested glory. All of these preceding testimonies were part of the original book first published in the year 2001, but God did not stop doing His wonders then. We decided to include here, in this enlarged and updated edition, some more recent testimonies to show what God is still doing today:

"In June of 2005, I was blessed by God to be introduced to Prophetess Andrea McDougal and her husband, and it was then that supernatural angelic manifestations began in our church and also in our individual lives.

"Thank God He led me to invite Prophetess Andy to be our special guest speaker at House of Praise (then located in Eagle Lake, Texas). As she was ministering on the subject of the Glory of God, supernatural miracles, signs and wonders began to occur among us. For one thing, feathers began falling from above. Just like that, out of the blue, they began drifting down very gracefully before our very eyes!

"Also, during the service, many people were heard to exclaim in awe at the gold dust that was appearing on their hands, faces, arms and Bibles and also on their seats, as the prophetess of the Lord was ministering.

"Our biggest amazement that evening came when a young girl of sixteen received a garnet toward the close of the service. We were all in worship before the Lord, and Hannah had her hands extended and raised to the Lord in worship. She later testified that she then felt something drop into the palm of her semi-cupped hand. Startled, she felt around with her pinky finger to be sure of what she was sensing. Sure enough there was something there. She brought her hand down to eye level, and, when she opened it, was amazed to find in it a beautiful red gemstone. It was beautifully faceted and reflected the light almost as if it were a living thing!

"Young Hannah was so astonished by this that she wept for joy. The words *amazement, wonder, humility, trembling* and *excitement* can only begin to express what she was feeling at that moment because of this miraculous event.

"When she first showed us the stone, we all thought it was a ruby, but we had it examined by two different jewelers, and they identified it as a garnet. Interestingly enough, Hannah was born in January, and that would make the garnet her birthstone. Of course, the Lord knew that.

"As Sister Andy prophesied an on-time and accurate word to our people, we sensed the power and presence of God heavily. Many were strengthened, healed, delivered and saved. I liked the way one man summed up this whole event, and his words still resound in my spirit. 'These manifestations,' he told us, 'are but a token of God's love for you.'

"And that was only the beginning. God began to manifest Himself in the personal lives of our members and to reveal Himself in their homes, their schools and their businesses as time went by.

"This has been a very humbling experience, and we sometimes ask the Lord, 'Why us?' We don't consider ourselves any more special than other churches, but we do believe that God can do anything. We count it a great blessing and an honor to be able to witness such marvels.

"And the angel feathers still continue to manifest, especially among the children and young people of the church. Those who visit our church are also experiencing signs and wonders of God's supernatural in their own homes, vehicles, and business places. Just a few days ago, Tuesday October 3, 2007, I was holding our eight-week-old son Joshua, and as I was getting ready to feed him, something began to swirl before us. It was a beautiful pink angel feather. This is an undeniable move of God and to Him be all the glory!"

Pastor David Jones
House of Praise
Katy, Texas

Concerning House of Praise in Katy, Texas

Our friends, Tommie Williams and Saundra Seale, were kind enough to introduce us to some of the churches they knew in the Houston area and arrange for us to minister there, and one of those churches was House of Praise (then located out in Eagle Lake). Because of the infamous Houston traffic, it took us quite some time to get to Eagle Lake that first night, but before we ever got there, God told me that the congregation and the pastor we were about to meet were marked for revival.

Eagle Lake seemed like a very odd place for revival to break out. Not only was it a small and remote place, rather hidden and secluded, but the church itself was located in an old car dealership on the edge of town.

We were pleasantly surprised about several things at House of Praise. There was a spirit of excellence in everything done there, and the people (all of them) were the most ardent worshipers we had seen in a long time. Everyone, old and young alike, was down front, singing and clapping and dancing before the Lord, and none was praising more exuberantly than their pastor, David Jones.

Also, the people were deeply respectful of each other and the Lord, and they were dead serious about their giving. These were all good signs.

When it came our time to minister, I declared what the Lord had told me. This congregation was marked for revival. God had a plan for how that would come to pass.

Pastor David invited us back on several occasions, and after several visits, I was led to teach one night on the glory. My text that night was from Isaiah 60, *"Arise and shine, for the glory of the Lord is risen upon you."* As the message progressed, golden angel feathers began to fall. It was phenomenal! At first, they were just in front, over me and the pastor, but then they began to fall over the congregation too.

It was while we were worshiping toward the end of the service that the gem appeared in the hand of Hannah (as previously related by Pastor Jones in his testimony). When I first saw the stone, I thought it was a garnet, but everyone was calling it a ruby. It turned out to be a garnet, as I had first thought. Garnets have a sort of golden color on the inside that makes them look as if a flame of fire is burning within. This one not only had that look, but in the days ahead, it grew.

To me, one of the most remarkable things about this stone is that it was perfectly faceted, as if a master jeweler had shaped it and made it ready to be placed in a beautiful setting. What a miracle! And it has now been seen by many.

Pastor David's office had been closed all during the service, and only he had the key. At the chose of the service, however, he found a feather on his desk.

Quite a few diamonds were found lying on the carpet in the sanctuary after the service had dismissed. In some of the services, there seemed to be a mist over the people, and some experienced what seemed like raindrops falling on them. In the days that followed, feathers of every size and color not only appeared in the services of House of Praise, but they also manifested in the people's homes, in their cars, in their places of business and even in the children's schools.

What's more remarkable is that this continues to happen today. Pastor David called me only a few days ago to report even more wonderful manifestations in the church and in his own home.

The result of all this was a catapulting of the church and its leader. Within months of these manifestations beginning, so many people were wanting to attend House of Praise that the Lord moved the congregation into Katy, a Houston suburb, and they have been outgrowing every location since then. Pastor David has since had his first book published (*Humble Is the Way,* Greenwell Springs, Louisiana: McDougal & Associates: 2007) and been on radio around the country and also on Christian television. God had marked them for revival, and He does what He promises.

Concerning Daytona City Church in Daytona Beach, Florida

Pastor Kathy Tolleson of Daytona City Church somehow got a copy of my book and read it, and when she did, her spirit was stirred, and she felt that the glory was something she and her people wanted more of. She was able to contact me and asked if we would be willing to come and do a ladies' conference she was organizing. We were happy to do it, even though it meant flying home from Paris one day and leaving for Daytona the next.

As it turned out, Pastors Rodney and Kathy Tolleson had a wonderful group of dedicated people who were very hungry for more of God. Leading up to the conference they had all put a lot of prayer and planning into making it a success, and their fear, as the moment approached, was that they would be disappointed, that for some reason God would not show up and reveal Himself as we had been experiencing elsewhere. They need not have worried. God did not disappoint them.

The conference was well attended and carried off with great professionalism and anointing. And God was there. No sooner had His Word begun to go forth than He began to reveal Himself with beautifully colored dustings of glory. That first day the keyboard and drums on the platform were covered with beautiful blue and purple dust, and the ministers seated on the platform saw gold dust appearing on their hands, faces, clothing and Bibles.

Pastor Kathy later testified that she had been wearing a sterling silver cross on a necklace, and when God began to manifest His glory, that silver cross turned gold. Likewise, someone was wearing silver colored shoes, and they were covered with gold dust.

Pastor Rodney's testimony was very different, but just as powerful. He had been teaching on The Heart of the Father. During the meetings he didn't experience the gold dust as many others had, and he wondered about that. When he went home that night and got undressed, he was surprised to see in a mirror that gold dust encircled his heart. To him, this was a confirmation of the truths he had been teaching.

ɘ

Concerning New Jerusalem Whole Truth Church in Humble, Texas

During the time we did several meetings in and around Houston, we were introduced to Pastors Lee and Pearl Gaddie of New Jerusalem Church of God in Humble, Texas and spoke for them. Pastor Gaddie invited us back to do several days of glory conference in his church. As always, no sooner had we begun to teach on God's glory than God began to confirm this word with signs following.

Angel feathers fell in our midst, and gold dust appeared on the people, but God had even greater things in store for us. The most remarkable miracle may have been reserved for a visiting pastor's wife.

Although many wonderful things happen as God's Word is going forth, the most unusual miracles are often reserved for later, during the time we are all worshiping Him together. And that's what happened in this case. As we all lifted our voices and our hands to God in worship, the Lord placed a beautiful stone in her hand.

In awe, she showed it to us, but as she did, it began to change. It seemed more like something living. It was pulsating, changing colors and growing before our very eyes. At the beginning it was clear. Then it changed to a pink. And eventually it was more of a red tone. Others who were present that night were able to see it forming, changing and manifesting. As we worship the King of Glory, the great I AM, Heaven opens over us.

I'm always reminded of the words of our great friend, Ruth Ward Heflin: "Praise until the spirit of worship comes. Worship until the glory comes. Then stand in the glory" (from her book *Glory,* Hagerstown, Maryland, McDougal Publishing: 1996.) It works. In previous years, we praised until the spirit of worship came, and then as we worshiped God together, prophecy came or some other manifestation. Now, we have entered into a deeper realm of the glory, Heaven is literally opened over us, and we are having experiences we've never had before.

Concerning Our Meetings with Pastors Allen and Debra Batiste in Houston, Texas

During that same period of time in which we met Pastors Gaddie in Humble and Pastors Jones in Eagle Lake, we were also introduced to Pastors Allen and Debra Batiste who had a church in South Houston. During the ministry of the Word, large pieces of gold dust blanketed the carpets in their sanctuary.

Concerning the Ministry of Pastor Sherlene Ivey in Fort Washington, Maryland

While attending a conference in Greenville, Texas, we met Pastor Sherlene Ivey of Fort Washington, Maryland, just outside of the nation's capital, and she invited us to do a week-long glory meeting in her place. During those meetings, God manifested Himself in various ways. Gemstones were often seen on the carpet as I sent forth the Word (they later disappeared). Feathers fell on the children. Gold dust appeared.

During that week of meetings, we stayed with Pastor Sherlene and her son James in her home. One day she came to our room and asked me to come see something. In her bedroom, lying on the carpet, was a beautiful ruby. It was a very exciting week!

Concerning our ministry with Pastors Yani and Natalie Ugani in Paris, France

Another person who read my book and wanted us to come for ministry was a Congolese pastor living and ministering in Paris. Pastor Yani and his lovely wife Natalie were desperately hungry for God to manifest His glory upon their people in Paris, people who were, for the most part, refugees from the troubled French speaking African nations. We agreed to go, and the people made great sacrifices to make the upcoming conference a success. And God didn't disappoint them.

As the people came forward for prayer, gold dust manifested on their hands, faces and clothes. It was a beautiful sight to behold.

To us, the most beautiful report came a few weeks after we had returned home. In one of their own services, the African pastors prayed for a child to be healed, and the child was covered from head to toe in gold dust. The Africans had become carriers of the glory.

Concerning our Ministry with Pastors Desmond and Mary Thomas in Freetown, Sierra Leone

A Bible school program had been organized some twenty years before at Bethel Temple in Freetown, Sierra Leone, West Africa. There were about twenty students in that course. One of those students, Desmond Thomas, went on to start two churches in Sierra Leone. Then, when war started in Sierra Leone, he moved to London, and there he organized and pastored another church among the African immigrants. Later, he began preaching here in our own country, and eventually he returned to Sierra Leone to start his own Bible college. Pastor Desmond was now ready to graduate his first class, sixty men and women ready for ministry, and he invited us to be the special speakers at the graduation, at a women's conference and at some other special meetings he organized at Bethel Temple. It was such a joy to participate in these historic meetings.

When the glory first began to manifest upon the hands of the Sierra Leoneans, for some reason, the light was so poor inside that it could not be seen. I encouraged them to go out into the sunlight and take another look. Sure enough, when they did this, a beautiful dusting of gold was visible upon their hands. It was a life-changing experience!

Concerning our Ministry in the
Glory Conference in Jerusalem

We were invited by Michael and Jane Nasrallah to be the special speakers at a glory conference in Jerusalem. At the time, they were living in Daytona and attending Daytona City Church, so Pastors Rodney and Kathy Tolleson and many of their people were along on this exciting trip.

There were a number of memorable things about the conference. While it was going on, we stayed in the heart of the Old City, and the church where the meetings were held was nearby, also in the Old City. That was a very special honor for me. Not only was it a city that God has long loved, but it was the home, for many years, of our dear friend, Ruth Ward Heflin, and her prayer ministry there on Mount Zion had changed the world.

To top it all off, God manifested His glory in that place with gold dust and angel feathers upon those who attended. That glorious presence then accompanied us as we toured other parts of Israel.

Other Books by Andy McDougal

HIS WONDERS IN THE DEEP

GOD'S CALL TO THE SUPERNATURAL

Andrea "Andy" McDougal

YOUR Camels Are Coming

The Bride's Journey to Destiny

Andrea "Andy" McDougal

The
ARROWS
of the
LORD

Andrea "Andy" McDougal

The

Power

of the

Seed

Andrea "Andy" McDougal

A Southern Lady's Tea Journey

A Legacy

Andrea "Andy" McDougal

A Southern Lady's Tea Adventures

Andrea "Andy" McDougal

Author Contact Page

You may contact Andy McDougal directly for conferences, retreats, missionary projects and church and house meetings. She is a gifted prophetess who will lift your people into the realms of glory.

18896 Greenwell Springs Road
Greenwell Springs, LA 70739

AndysMinistry@gmail.com

www.facebook.com/andrea.mcdougal.3
www.facebook.com/andymcdougalministries

Phone: 225-572-9844